BRITAIN'S LOST
CRICKET GROUNDS

BRITAIN'S LOST CRICKET GROUNDS

THE HALLOWED HOMES OF CRICKET THAT WILL NEVER SEE ANOTHER BALL BOWLED

CHRIS ARNOT

AURUM

To my wife, Jackie, and my daughters Katie, Suzi and Liz, who know nothing about cricket, my sons-in-law, who do, and my grandchildren who will do. Hopefully.

First published in Great Britain
2011 by Aurum Press Ltd
7 Greenland Street, London NW1 0ND
www.aurumpress.co.uk

A catalogue record for this book is available from the British Library.

ISBN 978 1 84513 591 1

10 9 8 7 6 5 4 3 2
2015 2014 2013 2012

Designed by Robert Updegraff
Printed in China

Front endpaper: Cricket Festival Week at the Crabble, Dover.

Back endpaper: Aerial view of the County Ground, Northlands Road, Southampton in the 1950s.

Half-title photograph: Castle Hill, Llanilar, Wales.

Title spread photograph: The Central Ground, Hastings, during the last-ever County Championship match played there by Sussex.

Contents spread: County Cricket Week at the Crabble Athletic Ground, Dover in the early 1900s.

ACKNOWLEDGEMENTS

A great many people have been very generous with their time to help make this book come together, whether providing memories, memorabilia or photographs: Dennis Amiss, Harold Rhodes, Jim Stewart, M.J.K. Smith, Jack Bannister, Ron Headley, Alan Oakman, Derek Underwood, David Allen, Jack Russell, Robin Hobbs, Neil Robinson, librarian at Lord's, Stephen Chalke, Brian Halford, cricket correspondent of the *Birmingham Post*, Pete Pritchard of Burton CC, Nick Shaw of Wymeswold CC, Tim Jones from Worcestershire CCC, Dave Allen from Hampshire CCC, Peter Wynne-Thomas of Nottinghamshire CCC, Patrick Talbot, Roger Davis of Oxfordshire Playing Fields Association, Roger Gibbons from Gloucestershire CCC, John Light, Ralph Wilkins, Eddie Cuss, Rob Broddie of Sussex CCC, Mark Foster of Hastings CC, Tony Debenham from Essex CCC, Stephen Skinner, secretary of Norfolk CCC, Duncan Hamilton, Chris Higginbottom, Philip Paine, Richard Cox of Stroud CC, John Lindley of Ealing CC, Douglas Miller, Brian Ryland, Dean Nelson, Martyn Johnson, Ernie Laister, Mike Murphy of Newstead Abbey CC, Roger Protz, Robin Varley, Kelsey Griffin of the Bletchley Park Trust, Robin Bowen-Williams, Peter Wigan of The Armadillos CC, Peter York, Peter French, Mark Foster of Hastings Priory CC, Ray Durrant, Mick Palmer, Robert Wainwright, Derek Lowe and Alan Forster from Skelmersdale CC, Andrew Hignell of Glamorgan CCC, Phillip Stallard of Newport CC, Mike Donnelly, Alistair Bolingbroke of Rochdale CC, John Raby, David Potter, Neil Leitch, historian of Cricket Scotland, Robert Jackson, David Lockwood of the *Huddersfield Examiner*, Stuart Machin, Rev. Malcolm Lorimer of Lancashire CCC, Mike Ulyatt, Frank Monks, Keith Donoghue, Harry Lewthwaite of the former Staveley CC, John Glaister, Mike Turner of Leicestershire CCC, John Coe of Hinckley Town CC, Mike Hall, Peter Lewis, Peter Tucker, Roger Neck of the Bristol and District Cricket League, Louise Cartledge, Gill Piercey, Roger Packham, Andrew Sowerby and Marion Allport of Littletown Parish Council, Graeme Weeks and Ron Young of the Durham Cricket Board, Andrew Vine and David Clay of the *Yorkshire Post*, Roger Mann, Anthony Burton, Kristina Watson of RCAHMS, David Scripps at Mirrorpix, Mark Vivian at Mary Evans.

Thanks also to Lydia Harley and Melissa Smith at Aurum for all their stalwart work in unearthing so many wonderful photographs, to my publisher Graham Coster for his advice and support and to Robert Updegraff for the book's design.

PICTURE CREDITS

Robin Varley 1, 70, 72 (top and bottom), 73, 74-75; Graham Morris, Cricketpix 2-3, 102-103, 105 (top) 183 (bottom); The Dover Society front endpapers, 6-7; Patrick Eagar 8, 21, 98, 101, 106-107; Dave Allen 9, 104, 105 (bottom); Mike Murphy 10 (top), 97; Roger Mann Collection 10 (bottom), 38 (bottom left), 58, 60, 100, 109, 138, 139 (top); 140, 150, 184, 185, 186, 187 (top), 188 (top and bottom), 189 (top and bottom), 190-191; Graham Coster 11, 92, 94; Getty Images 12, 15, 16-17, 22-3 (Adrian Murrell), 61 (top and bottom), 62-63; Alamy 14, 57, 89, 144 (bottom); Illustrated London News/Mary Evans Picture Library 18, 19, 20 (top), 40-41, 50, 142-143; Mark Foster 20 (bottom); Edale Society 24, 26; Chris Higginbottom 27 (top); Dean Nelson 28, 30, 35 (top); Mirrorpix 32-33, 34, 35 (bottom), 52-53, 82, 84, 118 (top), 122-123, 136 (top), 160, 162-163; Peter York 38-39, 39 (bottom right); John Player Archive, Nottingham City Museum and Galleries 42, 44-45; PA photos 48, 50, 54, 56 (top), ; Picture Sheffield 51, 56 (bottom); David Whitlock 64, 65 (top and bottom), 158, 159, 161 (top); Martyn Johnson 66 (top and bottom); Country Life Picture Library 68-69; Eddie Cuss 76-79; Yorkshire Post 85, 88; Co-operative Archive 90, 91; Don Mounsey 92; John Glaister 95; John Coe 108, ; Bletchley Park Trust 110, 112; Chris Arnot 113; Glamorgan Archives 118 (bottom); Brian Ryland 124, 125; Richard Cox 126 (top and bottom), 128, 129; Terry Bowler 130; Stephen Hodgkinson 135; Michael Palmer 136 (bottom); Dover Museum and Bronze Age Boat Gallery 139 (bottom); Bob Wainwright 141; Neil Leitch 144 (top); Alastair Allanach 146 (top and bottom), 147 (top); Tim Jones 148, 151; Diageo Archive 152,153; Craig Stoddart 154; Andrew Sowerby 156, 157; Phillip Paine 161 (bottom); David Relter 171; The Cricketer 172; John Raby 173; Alistair Bolingbroke 174, 176, 177 (top); Paul Gillett at www.geograph.co.uk 187; Bristol News and Media 164, 165, 166, 167 (top), 168-9; Bristol Record Office 167 (bottom); John Light 77, 78, 79; Derek Lowe 115, 117; Mike Ulyatt 82, 86, 87; David Frith back endpapers.

CONTENTS

INTRODUCTION

Imagine what it would have been like to be a spectator at the Central Ground, located on the idyllically named Priory Meadow in Hastings, one fine afternoon when Sussex were at home. To hear the cry of gulls hovering overhead or swooping on to the outfield before fleeing in a flap from a square cut cracked by Ted Dexter at his most imperious. To smell the whiff of briny on the breeze as Imran Khan hurtled in from the sea end. To see the sun's rays glinting on the windows of elegant boarding houses, their owners peering out anxiously as Tony Greig hit consecutive sixes from the first four balls of an over, including one that cleared the stand at square leg.

Sussex were playing Warwickshire on that occasion and, as one who spent his formative years at Edgbaston, I might have enjoyed the fifth ball of the same over even more. Greig was caught on the long-on boundary by Dennis Amiss for 226. Note the 'might have'. I wasn't there at the time, the mid-1970s. Nor did I see Dexter at Hastings in the 1960s or Imran in the 1980s. The first time I clapped eyes on the Central Ground was in the early 1990s, when it was already earmarked as the future site of a large shopping centre (named Priory Meadow, needless to say).

Now, you don't have to be a cricket fan to understand that this was a prime example of replacing the distinctive with the mediocre. Nor do you have to be a member of your local civic society to realise that this turn of events is hardly confined to Hastings. Developers and executives sitting in distant boardrooms have found it all too easy to push through plans for a multitude of soulless malls and precincts,

▲ The Central Ground, Hastings – now a shopping centre.

cavernous hypermarkets and edge-of-town retail parks harbouring identical chain stores. While nodding through their applications, toothless local authorities have devised traffic systems of byzantine complexity woven around traffic-free high streets laid out with identikit block paving and street furniture.

Cricket clubs have not been the only victims. Too many family-owned shops, characterful pubs and historic coaching inns have gone the same way. And sometimes cricket clubs have not been victims at all. The dedicated officials who run them have been willing to accept the developer's shilling as a way out of crippling debt. To make way for Tesco or Asda, Barratt or Bovis Homes, they upped stumps and moved. Often they acquired better facilities as a result, albeit in featureless settings, more often than not within corporately owned sports complexes. Some clubs went bust before developers, or anybody else, could make them an offer. Others lost manpower as well as money as players drifted away, seduced by the growing number of alternatives to spending weekend afternoons in the field or in the pavilion, and evenings in the club bar or the nearest pub.

The disappearance of distinctive cricket grounds didn't start in the 1980s; far from it. But the '80s speeded up the process. It was the decade when Britain changed, changed utterly. A terrible duty was born to rebalance the economy. Apparently there was no alternative but to allow mass manufacturing to wither while the commercial, retail and, above all, financial sectors were encouraged to bloom. The patronage that had given birth to country house cricket had largely died away decades before. Now the similarly enlightened self-interest that had bankrolled many a works cricket team began to disappear in turn.

▼ Derek Shackleton appeals in a Gillette Cup match against Kent in 1966. The batsman is Brian Luckhurst and Colin Ingleby-Mackenzie is behind the stumps, at Hampshire's County Ground in Northlands Road, Southampton – now a housing estate.

▼ New houses (far left) cover some of Newstead Colliery's old cricket ground; the rest remains as untended scrub.

Those paternalistic factory and brewery owners have long gone, as indeed have the dedicated groundsmen they employed. Colliery grounds began to disappear when the pits closed and a way of life was lost for ever. As the 1980s progressed, state school grounds were built on or given over to less time-consuming sports. And, as the 1980s gave way to the 1990s and the 1990s to the 2000s, sky-high house prices forced more and more youngsters to leave the villages they grew up in, depriving the cricket team of fresh talent in the process.

Each lost ground takes with it a little bit of England; or Wales, or Scotland, for that matter. But each lost ground has a story, stirring memories that have been kept alive long after the wicket disappeared under tarmac or bricks and mortar or the year-round pounding of football boots. Follow my meandering progress in search of those stories and we'll travel from Dover to Kirkcaldy, from Norwich to Newport, calling at overgrown fields, abandoned waste grounds, housing estates, supermarkets and car parks in between.

▼ The Angel Ground in Tonbridge in 1905 – now a shopping centre.

Don't worry. We won't be dwelling too long in the present. We'll be travelling back to times when these were the sites of cricketing deeds to stir the blood. Of demon bowlers and dashing batsmen, of bruising encounters, harsh words and

choice banter. Researching this book has been a 'labour of love', as my publisher promised it would be. I've met no end of genuine cricket devotees who have gone out of their way to help. Apologies to anyone I've omitted from the lengthy list of acknowledgements – a list that includes dedicated statisticians, stalwarts of club and village cricket, and a number of old pros, some of whom were among the sporting heroes of my childhood and youth.

Since their day, the professional game has changed beyond measure in a desperate attempt to appeal to a wider audience. But for some of us there is still a simple pleasure to be had, on a Saturday afternoon, in rounding a bend in a country lane and pulling over to watch for a while as thirteen men in white and two umpires follow the progress of a red ball around a green field on the edge of nowhere in particular. Yes, we have lost many a ground over the past half-century or so. Mercifully, however, there are still more than a few left to remind us that cricket is still threaded through the fabric and the folk memory of the country where this complex yet enthralling game has its roots. And hopefully we can assume that no shopping centres will be built on Broadhalfpenny Down in Hambledon.

▲ The Back Lane ground of Staveley Cricket Club in the Lake District, unused for twenty years and now richer in buttercups than runs.

▼ The arresting setting of the Royal High cricket ground at Holyrood in Edinburgh, seen from the top of Salisbury Crags, since built on by the Scottish Parliament.

A picturesque corner of the Cricket Ground.

BEDFORD HOTEL

REFRESHMENTS

Gunn before the sticks.

Some Reminiscences of the Hastings Festival.

Iohmann's favourite flourish after bowling.

1: HASTINGS

The seventeenth of January dawns wet and windy, appropriately enough. According to the BBC, this is officially the most miserable day of the year – a black Monday when the post-Christmas blues set in with a vengeance. Priory Meadow in Hastings is not a place to be on a day like this. Then again, for a cricket lover it's not a place to be on any day. What it represents is something all too common in the towns and cities of this sceptred isle – the replacement of something distinctive and full of character with an identikit example of every bog-standard shopping centre from here to Hull and beyond.

Priory Meadow was once the site of the Central Ground. Why so called? Because 'there cannot be a first-class ground in any town, anywhere else, that's more centrally situated', according to Gerald Brodribb, whose book, *Cricket at Hastings*, was published in 1989. That was the year that Sussex played their last County Championship match here, duly losing to Mike Gatting's Middlesex by nine wickets. Hastings Priory would continue with club cricket for another five years before moving to their new ground at the Horntye Sports Complex on a breezy cliff top.

By contrast, the Central Ground was once a natural harbour. It was close to the sea, yet sheltered from extreme coastal elements. Elegant four-storey Regency houses with wrought iron balconies peered loftily over the Alfred Coote stand, built above the Queen's Road shops in 1959. Rows of boarding houses clambered up the cliffs towards the castle ruins cresting the summit. Gulls soared overhead and John Arlott's claret-honed tones rose to new levels of lyricism as he set the scene for Sunday afternoon viewers during BBC2's coverage of John Player League matches.

It must have been some time in the early 1990s when I first clapped eyes on the Central Ground, unfiltered by television. We were visiting our friends the Leathers, whose son Nathaniel played here as a colt with Michael Yardy, later of Sussex and England. 'They're going to build on this,' said Nat's father, Peter.

◀◀ An 1892 poster advertising the Hastings cricket festival.

▶ The memorial to Priory Meadow's previous history as a cricket ground, at the shopping centre in Hastings that has been built over it.

'They're not!'

'They are.'

And they did. Twenty years later, I shelter under a glass canopy as the rain hammers down and water overflows the gutters, forming puddles on the paving stones that separate one row of chain stores from another. Between Thornton's and Vision Express is a cricketer cast in bronze. Just to rub it in, he's wearing a sun hat. As he stands on his toes and leans back to hook, he has managed to dislodge one of the bails. And the ball? Well, that's embedded in the upper floor frontage of a jeweller called F. Hinds, next door to Top Shop.

I've seen worse public sculptures, but what it represents is an all too typical developers' nod towards local sensibilities. It reminds me of the breweries who used to knock down well-loved pubs, replace them with red-brick boxes and then decorate the lounge bar with framed photos of the handsome coaching inn or colourfully tiled gin palace that they'd recently bulldozed.

I'm still musing on this when I spot the jaunty figure of Hastings Priory CC groundsman Mark Foster splashing through the puddles with his hand outstretched. So, Mark, is that statue sited roughly where the wicket was? 'Nowhere near it,' he says and leads the way into a covered mall. He comes to a halt between Boots and River Island before proclaiming: 'This was about it, if you're talking about the track used for first-team and county matches. And that was the South Terrace end,' he adds with a glance back over his shoulder. To the fore is the English Channel. 'I remember watching Imran Khan steaming in from the sea end,' he goes on. 'His run-up seemed to cover three-quarters of the outfield.'

To find the site of the 'new' pavilion, built in 1935, we have to walk beyond Dorothy Perkins and take the lift to the first floor. 'That's roughly where it was,' says Mark, gesturing at what is now the Cheeky Monkeys Creche. The old pavilion, nestling in the shadow of a handsome row of tall town houses, was built in 1884. A century later and the players were still taking tea there. 'Facilities were pretty basic in both pavilions compared to what we've got now,' Mark confides.

He started work at the Central Ground straight from school in 1980 under the guidance of Jim Case, one of a long line of Hastings groundsmen who stood no nonsense. One Alf Tutt started here in 1902 and stayed for fifty years. He used to bark through a megaphone at anyone straying near a wicket once described by W.G. Grace, no less, as 'the truest piece of turf in the United Kingdom'. Heaven knows how Tutt

◀ The captains for the South of England v Australia match played at Hastings in September 1905 – Joseph Darling, Australia (left) posing with Dr. W.G. Grace.

Rows of boarding houses clambered up the cliffs from the Central Ground towards the castle ruins. This view is from 1910.

would have addressed the German airmen who had the effrontery to drop five bombs on the Central Ground in July 1940. 'Fortunately, they avoided the square,' Brodribb writes, going on to point out that the Germans must have had an out-of-date map. They apparently thought that they'd successfully bombed Hastings harbour.

Two years after the war ended, crowds flocked to the Central Ground for the end-of-season Cricket Week and the local derby with Kent. Those who were also lucky enough to be there for the match between the South Africans and a South of England XI saw Denis Compton break Sir Jack Hobbs's long-standing record by completing his seventeenth century of the summer with the second ball after tea. Photographers piled on to the field and the celebrations lasted for five minutes. When the innings resumed, Compton strode down the wicket to Mann and was promptly stumped for 101.

Forty summers previously, Gilbert Jessop had provided even richer entertainment by hitting 191 in ninety minutes for the Gentlemen of the South against the Players of the South. The innings included thirty fours and five sixes at a time when the umpire would only raise both arms if the ball went out of the ground. One landed among the cabs lined up outside the town hall, putting the fear of God into the horses. Another landed on a roof in Station Road, where it remained. Yet another smashed the window of a chapel. In between times, he managed to 'scatter the ladies sitting near Mr de Cross's marquee', according to one eye witness.

There must have been something in the seaside air at Hastings that encouraged batsmen to throw caution to the wind. Maurice Tate, who regarded this as his favourite ground, wrote of Cricket Week, 1935: 'Never since I have been playing for Sussex have I seen so many sixes at the Central Ground. Some were tremendous swipes.' No mean swiper himself, Tate had been known to deposit balls into Queen's Road and into the elevated gardens of Devonshire Road, causing several long-distance spectators to leap from their deck chairs.

In 1975, Tony Greig hit one over square leg that landed on the small penthouse roof of the Alfred Coote stand and bounced into Queen's Road – bearing in mind that the stand was 31ft high and the shop fronts were 110 yards from the wicket. It was Greig's fourth consecutive six from the off-breaks of Peter Lewington of Warwickshire. Going for a fifth, he was caught on the long-on boundary by Dennis Amis for 226.

Greig had been in a rather turbulent Sussex dressing room in 1968 when Ted Dexter marked his return after a long absence with a double century at Hastings. 'I can't vouch for its authenticity,' Greig told Alan Lee, author of Lord Ted, 'but the story goes that our twelfth man was sent out from the ground to clear a runway of sorts so that Ted could land his private plane. When he strode into the dressing room, a strange smell accompanied him. It was his cricket case, unchanged from three years of semi-retirement and suffering from mould and dry rot.'

There was nothing mouldy about Dexter's batting as he set about Kent's Derek Underwood with some gusto – not normally advisable on any pitch, and particularly not at Hastings. 'It was usually a very special place for me,' Underwood told me, 'and I was naturally very disappointed when I heard that they were going to build on it. All my best achievements seem to have been at Hastings. I remember taking 9 for 28 against Sussex in 1964. That remains my best bowling analysis. And I got my only first-class century at the Central Ground. That must have been twenty years later.'

Indeed it was. In a Costa coffee bar at Priory Meadow, Mark Foster delves into his rucksack and pulls out a clutch of newspaper cuttings. 'Deadly Derek finally gets that ton at 39', reads the headline in the *Daily Mirror* from 3 July 1984. Even more remarkably, the three-day match was eventually tied. On the previous day, Underwood had taken 6 for 12 in a John Player League match. No wonder he liked Hastings. 'Towards the end, I think Kent and their supporters enjoyed coming here more than Sussex did,' Mark muses. 'We're only just over the county border and away teams stayed overnight. They didn't have to drive backwards and forwards along the A27 every morning and evening.'

The road was rather less congested in Alan Oakman's heyday, the 1950s and '60s. The rangy all-rounder plied his trade at Hove, for the most part, but he was a Hastings man born and bred. 'At thirteen or fourteen you don't realise how lucky you are,' he reflects at his current home in a leafy part of Birmingham. 'I went to the grammar school in Hastings and learnt my cricket at the Central Ground. It was a lovely place to play.' Although there were occasions, he recalls, when sun stopped play. Eh? 'We used to start at eleven thirty in those days and sometimes the sun's rays used to hit a glass roof and reflect back at the batsman. If that happened, we'd take an early lunch around twelve thirty.' No designer shades for that generation of cricketers, thank you very much. 'It was a good cricketing pitch,' Alan continues. 'Did a bit in the first hour, then it was good for batting between lunch and tea. Hastings Cricket Week was supposed to be like Scarborough, but it never made as much money. I remember our [Sussex's] secretary saying that we could make more money on a wet day at Hove than a sunny day at Hastings. Why? Because the members lived locally.'

▼ Denis Compton turns a ball from spinner Jim Laker (out of picture) off his legs to score another boundary past the despairing reach of the short leg fielder as wicketkeeper Stewart 'Billy' Griffith looks on. Compton was playing for 'The South' against 'Sir Pelham Warner's Eleven' at the Central Recreation Ground, Hastings. During the match he passed the record for number of runs scored in a first class season previously held by Tom Hayward.

And, needless to say, it was money that ultimately sealed the Central Ground's fate at a time when all counties were looking to cut their commitment to out grounds and consolidate their finances.

The battle for Hastings's soul began in 1982. Sam Chippendale was one of the partners behind the Arndale centres and a man who seemed hell-bent on turning the UK into one giant shopping mall. He duly approached Hastings Borough Council with a proposal. 'But he didn't realise that the ground was privately owned and he'd have to come to us,' says Graeme Mounsey, Hastings Priory chairman for thirty years and now treasurer. 'The land had been sold to the trustees by the Cornwallis family in 1851.'

But surely that land was left to the people of Hastings in perpetuity. 'It was,' the treasurer concedes. 'I had meetings with old Lord Cornwallis, who has since died, and the charity commissioners. I managed to convince them that what we were planning was in the best interests of the trust.'

Graeme is seventy-seven. In his youth he played for Hastings and for Sussex seconds. 'As a teenager I saw Bradman's Australians at the Central Ground,' he says. 'It was a lovely place for cricket.' So why would you want to sell it to developers?

'My heart said no but my head said yes. The ground was very old. The buildings were falling down. It flooded regularly and we couldn't use it in winter. We were offered a new ground with facilities for football and other sports and a [£5 million] lottery grant.'

▲ Denis Compton acknowledges the crowd at the Central Recreation Ground, Hastings in 1947, having beaten Jack Hobbs' record of sixteen centuries in a season.

▶ One groundsman and his dog. Len Creese was so good at his job that he was lured away to Hove, only to be called back when the Hastings wicket deteriorated so much that county cricket was temporarily suspended.

As the 1980s wore on, the arguments raged and a public inquiry was held. But by the end of the decade, the outcome was inevitable. Brodribb was aware of that when he wrote his final lines:

'The sea is near: the channel winds blow up from the west and bring the screaming gulls: they swoop on the outfield until the ball hurries them away. There is shelter in this enclosed arena with its terraced walls of houses, and the slanting sunlight shines off the distant windows. High above, the ruined castle looks down upon this intimate oasis of peace amid the busy town. But not for long now. I cannot be the only one who feels that the passing of this unique ground hurts like the loss of a dear friend.'

You don't have to come from Hastings to sympathise with those sentiments. You just have to be a cricket lover contemplating the Priory Meadow shopping centre on a wet Monday morning.

Members take full advantage of a sunny day at the seaside for Sussex's final County Championship match at the County Ground.

Wrought iron balconies offering fine views of the day's play at Priory Meadow for residents and guests.

2: EDALE

Isaac Cooper shared his surname with most of the village team at Edale. Fathers and sons, uncles and nephews played together. Isaac was the groundsman and not one to be messed with. 'To me he was Uncle Isaac, and he'd chase us off with a shovel if we encroached on his pitch,' recalls Roger Cooper, who was ten in 1955 when cricket was coming to an end on what must have been one of the steepest pitches in England. Well, flat ground is at something of a premium in the Derbyshire Peaks and, having nurtured a cricket square in what was essentially a sloping farmer's field, Isaac was determined to defend it against all-comers.

That included cows as well as small children. 'They had to stop the game when the farmer brought them in for milking and stand guard in case one of them strayed from the herd and trampled over the wicket. During the week it was protected by a temporary fence,' Roger goes on.

These days he runs Cooper's Camp Site. There's a stand pipe right in the middle of Uncle Isaac's beloved pitch and the outfield is covered with tents and caravans. Demand for space increased as the 1950s faded and the leisure industry expanded. The old railway carriage that doubled as a pavilion is long gone, but the café where the teams took tea is still there. Cricket had been played on the site since the 1880s and memories of its communal role in a very different rural England emerge every now and then. 'We found a shield with a cricket ball embedded in it when we were clearing out my dad's house,' Roger confides. 'He was presented with it after taking a hat-trick.'

The clearing of Edward Cooper's house also unearthed a photo of cricket resuming at Edale in 1945, after the end of the Second World War. Edward's nephew Brian Cooper, now eighty-seven, had just been demobbed from the Fleet Air Arm and was exercising his formidable bowling arm again after a few wartime games in Gibraltar. The teenager who had terrorised more than a few visiting teams had grown into a

◀◀ ▲ The Edale cricket team of 1905.

◀◀ ▼ Cricket resumes after the Second World War at Cooper's Field in the Peak District in a setting that must have seemed forever England.

▲ The Edale team of 1921.

man. 'When the surface wasn't kind, you could get them to lift a bit past their ear-'oles,' he recalls. 'It wasn't appreciated by the batsmen, but it did make them apprehensive about the next delivery.'

Brian would go on to play well into his fifties and take over 1,000 wickets in the Derbyshire and Cheshire League, first for New Mills and then for Chapel en le Frith. But Edale was his cricketing cradle – as indeed it was for his younger brother Norman Cooper, eventually a wicketkeeper-batsman, who joined the team two years before being called up for National Service. 'I started as a long stop because we had a useless wicketkeeper,' he chuckles. He happened to be one of the few non-Coopers in the team, but then he would have required the agility of an Olympic gymnast to cope with brother Brian's rising deliveries. More often than not, it seems, they flew past the keeper's ear-'oles as well as the batsman's.

Mercifully, perhaps, Brian was never unleashed running downhill. As Simon Lacey, Chris Higginbottom and Tom Whittington reveal in their post-war survey of *Derbyshire Cricket Grounds*, 'the considerable slope meant that wickets were pitched across the field and the straight boundaries were minuscule because the field is less than 70 yards wide.'

It was, by all accounts, an easy ground on which to hit a straight six, although not advisable to try it when Brian Cooper had ball in hand. Other bowlers' deliveries would disappear into the adjoining meadow at regular intervals. 'The grass was quite long,' Roger Cooper remembers, 'and we young lads had to spend a lot of time in there looking for the ball.'

Best place for them as far as Uncle Isaac was concerned.

◀ The Coopers' family field as it is today in a very different England.

EDALE

27

◀ An Edale youth team in the 1950s.

3: COURTAULDS

Mr Whippy is parked outside what was once The Crow in the Oak pub and is now the Copacabana Bar and Restaurant. A pale and spotty youth bites into the chocolate flake of his 99-er and points me in the direction of a gate between a Sikh temple and a company called Essential Party Hire ('balloons, decorations and crockery a speciality'). The gate, padlocked and topped by rusting barbed wire, is at the far end of a nearby car park, pitted with pot-holes. 'Please be aware of pickpockets,' says a sign by the gate. 'They are watching you.' I'm more conscious of being under surveillance by several closed circuit cameras as I peer through the railings of the gate at an all too depressing sight. Was this the place that launched a thousand clips – off the legs and over a short-ish mid-wicket boundary?

Indeed it was. Because this was once the Courtaulds ground in Coventry, the grandest, best-kept works ground in a city that was strewn with them. Warwickshire played here twice a season most years between 1949 and 1982. It was in that final season that a youthful Gladstone Small was no-balled ten times in one over against Middlesex. 'Desperately trying to complete it, Small walked in off two paces – and bowled a wide,' Simon Hughes recalls. Four years later, Small was playing for England. By then he was already a cult figure at Edgbaston and it would have been quite under-standable if he had hoped never again to be sent to Coventry.

Other Warwickshire players felt differently, particularly those from earlier genera-tions who relished playing county cricket in front of a crowd that seemed closely packed together after the wide open spaces of a three-quarters empty Test arena.

The Courtaulds pavilion alone cost £15,000 in 1935. Gone, all gone. Apart, that is, from a low stretch of brick wall that may or may not have formed part of the founda-tions. Weeds and brambles grow in profusion around a gravel path that still encircles a sizeable patch of grass. At least it has been mown in recent times, although no cricket

◀◀ The boarded-up remains of the pavilion at what's left of what was once the finest of many works cricket grounds in Coventry.

square is discernible. Car boot sales are apparently staged here on Sundays, according to a sign in another car park beyond the Mercia Leisure Centre and Banqueting Suite. This used to be the Courtaulds Sports and Social Club in the days when the nearby factory employed around 5,000 staff. By 1992 the numbers had dwindled to 450. Closure finally came in 2007. But the rot had set in back in the early 1980s when Coventry's manufacturing base was devastated by recession.

The view is no better from the other side of the banqueting suite. Beneath locked, spiked gates a blue and white tape, of the sort used by police to seal off a crime scene, is rustling in the breeze. It would be trite to say that what lies beyond those gates is a crime against cricket. Economic upheaval and social change brought it about. Simple as that. Here are more brambles, more weeds, another gravel path to nowhere. Fifty yards along it, a discarded chair lies flat on its back as though contemplating the leaden skies above.

▼ 'You could see everything about the fielders; they almost trod on you' – Tom Cartwright on watching cricket while sitting on the grass he would later grace as a player.

Enough of this morbid dwelling on the present. Let's roll back those clouds and roll back the years to the days when first-class cricketers came to town and female employees would crane their necks out of the window of the Courtaulds laboratory to catch sight of them. To 1957, perhaps, when Brian Statham took fifteen wickets here for Lancashire. Or 1970 when Rohan Kanhai hit a blistering 187 not out for the home side against Derbyshire; or 1973 when Barry Richards stroked 240 for Hampshire in one day.

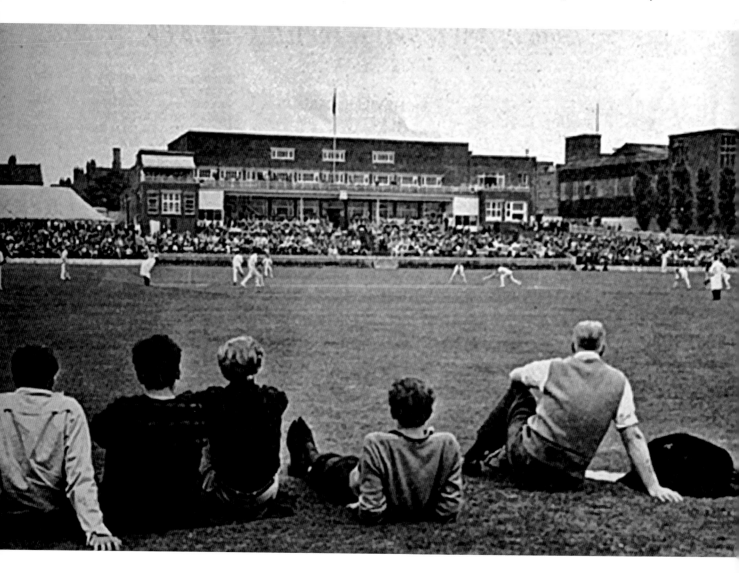

▲ Coventry crowds were always 'sizeable and appreciative' in Dennis Amiss's day.

Coventry-born Ian Chadband, now the chief sports correspondent of the *Daily Telegraph*, had taken the day off school to see his hero, and the dashing South African didn't disappoint. 'I'd watched him on televised John Player matches on a Sunday afternoon and he'd really caught my imagination,' Chadband recalls. 'He made the game look ridiculously easy. At Courtaulds that day he hit thirty-eight fours and three sixes.'

Did any of those sixes, one wonders, land in one or another of the back gardens that bordered the ground on the far side from the clubhouse? And were there occasions when a householder tending his herbaceous border or vegetable patch was approached by a county outfielder enquiring politely: 'Can we have our ball back?'

Dennis Amiss, who hit centuries himself on this ground in 1967, '72 and '76, never had to do that. 'The balls would come back eventually, but not always straight away,' he remembers. 'We always had to carry a box of spares with us whenever we went to Courtaulds.' Particularly, it would seem, when Kanhai was at the wicket. Dennis remembers that undefeated 187 with something approaching awe. 'Bill Blenkiron was keeping up the other end and I think he made about twenty out of a stand of 170 with Rohan.'

Amiss enjoyed being sent to Coventry. 'They always made us very welcome and the lunches were particularly good. The Lord Mayor usually turned up at some point and the crowds were sizeable and appreciative – at least they seemed sizeable because they were more packed in than they would have been at Edgbaston.'

Warwickshire play Surrey at Courtaulds in July 1966.

For two other Warwickshire stalwarts, Tom Cartwright and Jim Stewart, going to Courtaulds was like going home. They were what are known in these parts as 'Coventry kids'. After playing together for Coventry Schools in 1950, they'd graduated to work at the Rootes motor company – Jim on the Hillman Minx and Tom on the Humber Super Snipe. Neither would stay factory-bound for long. They were already making their way through the local leagues while dreams of playing for the county club up the road in Birmingham sustained them through the tedium of track work. Courtaulds played a special part in sustaining those dreams. In his biography of Cartwright, Stephen Chalke quotes the highly regarded all-rounder on what it was like to watch cricket there as a boy: 'You could see everything about the fielders; they almost trod on you. In the intervals we'd play cricket with a bottle and a tennis ball. And at 5.30 people from all the car factories would come down the path between the works and the pavilion and stand seven or eight deep, watching.' On the first day of the first county match in the summer of '63, all eyes were on Cartwright the man as he took eight Hampshire wickets for 45 on his home-town turf.

Stewart was already playing in the nets with Courtaulds' senior players when he was just thirteen. Twelve years later, in 1959, he would hit 159 for Warwickshire against Essex. Jim was a big hitter if ever there was one. So did he bombard those gardens? 'I must have hit a few sixes in that innings,' he says, 'but I don't remember breaking any windows. Those short boundaries resulted in a lot of catches because the rope seemed so near and batsmen had a go when they ought to have been more circumspect.'

I ask him about the most terrifying bowler he ever faced on a ground that must have seemed quite tight for one who plied his trade at Edgbaston. 'Tyson,' he replies without hesitation. 'I noticed the wicketkeeper disappearing into the middle distance until he was ten yards from the boundary as Frank started his run-up. He was difficult to play against on any ground.'

After retirement, Jim kept a couple of sports shops in Coventry, one of them almost within window-smashing range of the Courtaulds ground. It's not there now, I notice as I walk back to the car and Mr Whippy's chime starts up like a flat and tinny requiem for long-ago summers.

 Warwickshire play Surrey at Courtaulds in July 1966.

THE WARWICKSHIRE COUNTY CRICKET CLUB

WARWICKSHIRE
-v-
MIDDLESEX

at Courtaulds Ground, Coventry
on
August 7th., 9th. & 10th., 1971

3p.

* Captain
† Wicketkeeper

BONUS POINTS TO DATE
HOME TEAM...... *122+*
VISITORS...... *27+*

A new ball may be taken after 85 overs

HOURS OF PLAY (Subject to alteration) First two days 11.30 a.m. to 6.30 p.m. Third day 11 a.m. to 5.30 or 6 p.m.
LUNCH 1.30 p.m. to 2.10 p.m.
TEA INTERVAL (20 minutes) 4.15 p.m.

WARWICKSHIRE	1st INNINGS		2nd INNINGS	
1. J. WHITEHOUSE	c Brearley b Black	13	b Titmus	8
2. R.N. ABBERLEY	c Murray b Black	0	b Titmus	12
3. R. KANHAI	lbw Jones	5		
4. M.J.K. SMITH	c Smith b Jones	78		
5. D.L. AMISS	c Murray b Jones	17		
6. E.E. HEMMINGS	b Edmonds	23		
7. K. IBADULLA	c sub. b Jones	52		
8. N. McVICKER	c Titmus b Jones	1	not out	1
9. A.C. SMITH	b Edmonds	5	not out	0
10. S.J. ROUSE	b Jones	7		
11. L.R. GIBBS	not out	0		
	Extras	16	Extras	4
	Total	217	Total	25-2

UMPIRES W.E. PHILLIPSON. P.B. WIGHT.

1 wkt for–1 2–13 3–20 4–62 5–112 6–196 7–200 8–200 9–217 10–217
1 wkt for–2+ 2–25 3– 4– 5– 6– 7– 8– 9– 10–

Bowling Analysis (MIDDLESEX)	O	M	R	W	Nb	Wd	O	M	R	W	Nb	Wd
Black	20	4	39	1								
Jones	31	13	52	7								
Titmus	28	7	54	0								
Edmonds	19	4	47	2								
Featherstone	5	1	9	0								

MIDDLESEX	1st INNINGS		2nd INNINGS	
1. W.E. RUSSELL	b McVicker	1		
2. M.J. SMITH	lbw b Rouse	18		
3. P.A. PARFITT	c A.C.Smith b Ibadulla	5		
* 4. J.M. BREARLEY	c M.K.Smith b Gibbs	0		
5. C.T. RADLEY	c Whitehouse b Gibbs	38		
6. N. FEATHERSTONE	lbw Gibbs	86		
† 7. J.T. MURRAY	c + b Gibbs	31		
8. C.J. BLACK	b Gibbs	11		
9. K.V. JONES	b McVicker	15		
10. F.J. TITMUS	not out	2		
11. P.H. EDMONDS	b Ibadulla	12		
	Extras	12	Extras	
	Total	257	Total	

SCORERS P. PIKE. J. SIMMS.

1 wkt for– 2 2–37 3–5(4–66 5–6) 6–176 7–202 8–205 9– 10–
1 wkt for– 2– 3– 4– 5– 6– 7– 8– 9– 10–

Bowling Analysis (WARWICKS.)	O	M	R	W	Nb	Wd	O	M	R	W	Nb	Wd
McVicker	23	4	52	2								
Rouse	20	2	48	1								
Ibadulla	21	7	63	2								
Gibbs	29.2	9	70	5								
Hemmings	12	3	22	0								

WARWICKSHIRE won the toss and elected to BAT.

A scorecard from Warwickshire's match against Middlesex in August 1971.

Warwickshire play Surrey at Courtaulds in July 1966.

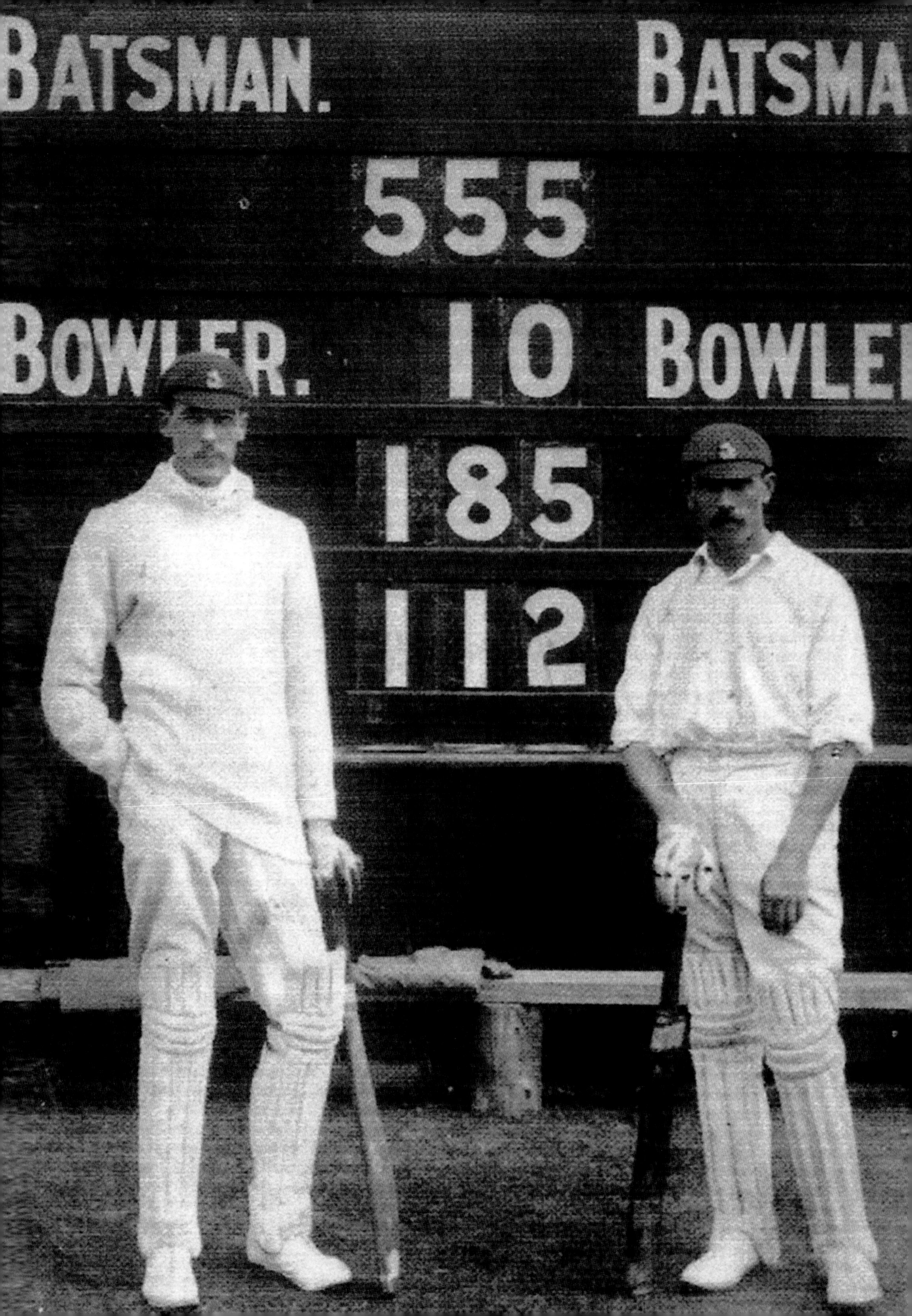
BATSMAN.
BATSMA
555
BOWLER.
10
BOWLEI
185
112

4: TONBRIDGE

Frank Woolley could empty Tonbridge High Street. All he had to do was stride from the pavilion across the nearby Angel Ground and take guard for Kent. The word would spread around the shops: 'Woolley's at the wicket.' Tobacconists and butchers would bolt their doors and not expect to reopen any time soon. One of the great run accumulators of English cricket tended to command the crease for some time. 'There was all summer in a stroke by Woolley,' wrote R.C. Robertson-Glasgow, 'and he batted as it is sometimes shown in dreams.' He could bowl a bit too, sharing the spoils with Colin Blythe when Kent dismissed Warwickshire here for just 16 in 1909.

Woolley was a local boy. His parents kept a cycle and small machinery repair shop that has long since evolved into yet another outpost of Starbucks. At least there's a blue plaque to commemorate the great all-rounder embedded in the brickwork above the front window. 'He hit the first of his 145 first-class centuries just across the road in 1906,' says Peter French, president of Tonbridge Cricket Club. We pause to pay our respects before wandering up the street to look at the site of the Angel Hotel, where the players used to stay. It's now a branch of Pound Stretcher.

And the Angel Ground itself?

To get to that we walk back through a shopping mall called, almost inevitably, The Pavilion – although the real pavilion was diagonally across a vast car park at what is now a Kwik Fit tyre repair outlet. Peter is a sprightly seventy-three and remembers playing football at the Angel in a couple of Tonbridge League cup finals back in the 1960s. Not cricket, though.

◀◀ Frank Woolley (left) and Arthur Fielder in front of the scoreboard at the Angel Ground in Tonbridge, registering their last wicket stand of 235 to beat Worcestershire in 1909.

▼ The scorecard from 1909 when Warwickshire were dismissed for 16.

◀ Tonbridge Cricket Week, 1902, painted by Mike Insley and now hanging in the Angel Centre.

You'd have to be fairly long in the tooth to remember watching a game at here, let alone playing in it. The last match was in 1942, when German aircraft, returning from a raid over London, jettisoned their remaining bombs over Tonbridge.

'The army requisitioned the ground after that and used it for storage,' Peter recounts, having consulted the club history at the current ground, Poplar Meadow, a mile and a half away. So what happened after the war? 'Well, by no means all the players came back and the pitch was in a poor state. The club sold the land for £7,000 to a company that wanted to convert it into a dog track. But that never got off the ground, so the local council bought it and leased it to Tonbridge Angels FC.'

Then came the retail boom of the 1980s and – you've guessed it – the local authority sold it to developers for £1.75 million. 'Imagine if we'd still owned the freehold,' says the president wistfully. Don't dwell on it, Peter. That way mad-

◀◀ A Kent match at the Angel Ground in 1901, before the ground was requisitioned by the army during the Second World War.

◀ A fine vantage point from which to watch Woolley. This shop's two balconies would be much in demand when Kent came to town to play at the Angel Ground.

A County Championship match between Kent and Sussex at the Angel Ground. The famous Indian player, K.S.Ranjitsinhji is at the crease for Sussex, facing the bowling of A.Hearne, with C.B. Fry the batsman at the non-striker's end. Ranjitsinhji scored 192 not out in his innings and in doing so passed 1000 runs for the season. The match was drawn.

ness lies. Instead we stroll over to the point where the frontage of Sainsbury's adjoins a department store called Beale's. Just above a window display of handbags is another plaque, unveiled by Chris Cowdrey in 1986, to mark the rough location of the Angel Ground wicket. Next to it is a sign forbidding skateboarding.

More memories are to be found in the nearby Angel Centre, an indoor sports complex. Near the front door is a handsome painting of Tonbridge Cricket Week, 1902, by Mike Insley, next to an evocative photograph of the following year's visit by the county team. It was evidently a major event in the local calendar, judging by the

crowds around the boundary. By no means all present are watching the cricket. Picnickers are lounging on the grass. Ladies are parading with parasols.

Peter and I adjourn to a nearby table where he pulls out a few pictures of his own. One shows the old wooden pavilion with its long, sloping roof at the rear, like a ski run. On the other, two locally born players lean on their bats in front of a scoreboard registering 555. It marked a record last-wicket stand of 235 by Kent to beat Worcestershire in July 1909. One was Arthur Fielder; the other – need you ask – was Frank Woolley.

5: JOHN PLAYER

There was a time when BBC Television gave to cricket more air time than brief Test match highlights at the end of the news. In the 1970s BBC2 devoted whole Sunday afternoons to John Player League matches. Jim Laker provided expert summary and commentary came from John Arlott, that reassuringly familiar voice honed by vintage claret but not by the pipe tobacco that he advertised on another channel. As for John Player, the company was able to promote its products through cricket in a way that would be unthinkable in today's more health-conscious climate.

On the site of its sports ground in Nottingham stands an enormous David Lloyd fitness centre offering just about every sport imaginable. Apart from cricket, that is. Where is the handsome half-timbered pavilion? Well, it could be where the outdoor tennis courts now stand. Or was it where those football pitches are – or the squash courts, or the hairdressers, or the children's nursery? Nobody seems to know; not even the bloke in the bobble hat nursing a cappuccino in a cup the size of a soup bowl who says he once saw Bob Willis playing for Surrey here back in 1971, shortly before his move to Warwickshire. 'All I can remember is the length of his curving run-up,' he says. 'He seemed to start out on the ring road.' That would be Western Boulevard, a name which makes a busy dual carriageway sound more exotic than it is. You can hear the traffic thundering by beyond the trees that fringe what is now the site of the tennis courts.

The cricket ground hosted four Sunday league games in the early 1970s and three women's one-day internationals in the 1990s. Notts' second XI played many a match

▲ The handsome pavilion at the John Player Ground in Nottingham.

here as well. It was opened in 1906 for John Player employees based at a factory just down the road in Alan Sillitoe country – the inner-city suburb of Radford that inspired *Saturday Night and Sunday Morning*.

For now let's stick with Sunday afternoons. Nottinghamshire is blessed with one of England's finest Test grounds. So why would the club want to abandon the splendours of Trent Bridge to play forty-over matches at what was nothing more than an admittedly well-appointed works ground across the river and round the ring road?

'In those days we used to play at places such as Worksop and Cleethorpes, so it was thought diplomatic that we should occasionally put in an appearance at the ground owned by the company sponsoring the Sunday league,' says former batsman and sometime wicketkeeper Sheik Basharat Hassan, better known as 'Basher'. He remembers one game in particular. It was 1970 and, with South Africa ostracised from Test cricket as the anti-apartheid movement gathered momentum, England were playing the Rest of the World at Trent Bridge on 2, 3, 4, 6 and 7 July. The missing day, 5 July, was a Sunday and therefore a rest day. Well, restful for some. It was also John Player League day and Notts were due to entertain Hampshire at the ground that carried the sponsor's name.

The incomparable Gary Sobers was captaining the world side. He was also a Notts player. For one reason or another, however, he didn't make the trip across the city to play on that Sunday. South African-born Barry Richards did turn out for Hants and perhaps wished that he hadn't. 'He was hit on the thumb by a rising ball from Barry Stead that put him out of the Trent Bridge game for the last two days,' Basher recalls. 'I'd been named as twelfth man so I stood in for him in the field.' At least that Sunday afternoon game at the John Player ground gave him some time in the middle, where he hit a brisk 77. Mike Harris topped it with 104 not out and Notts won by 34.

'It was a good pitch,' Basher recalls, 'and a fine pavilion with a big dressing room, more than adequate showers and a dining room offering a good lunch.' Any cigarettes? 'Each team was given two hundred before any of those games. As I recall, Barry Stead nicked most of them. He smoked like a chimney.'

Sadly, he died of cancer when he was forty.

▼ A women's cricket World Cup match between India and West Indies at the John Player Cricket Club in Nottingham in July 1993. Pramila Bhat limbers up.

A superb aerial view of the John Player Athletic Ground showing the array of cricket pitches.

6: CHACOMBE

Early lunchtime in the George and Dragon at Chacombe, a short ride from Banbury Cross, and three former members of the village cricket team are about to retrace their steps to the ground that they graced on many a summer Saturday. In their heyday, the 1970s and 1980s, they would be striding thirstily in the other direction at close of play. Home team and opponents would cram into the snug to carouse and sing long into the night.

The snug has long gone. A pub that dates back to the Domesday Book has been modernised and gentrified with a menu of modern British cuisine and a dining area to match. The cricket ground has gone too. Today it's just another field, bordered on one side by the manor house moat and on the other by a ditch marking the boundary between Northamptonshire and Oxfordshire. 'Hit it hard enough and you could get it into the next county,' smiles Graham Watts, sixty-one, one of many a Watts to have played here on the Northants side of the boundary. Not all of them are related, but in Graham's case, both his father and son turned out for the village team.

'A lot of fathers and sons played together,' says Roger Davis, former village postmaster and another Chacombe stalwart. There were rather more fathers than sons by 2002, when the team made headlines in the *Daily Telegraph* by recording a score of just 3, including eight ducks, in a match in May against Marston St Lawrence. 'The shrouds were almost on by then,' Roger, now sixty-five, reflects. 'The team packed up the following year.' He still has a framed copy of the *Telegraph* piece, which he holds up in the George and Dragon to much amusement. Behind the laughter, though, is a serious point that extends far beyond the borders of Northamptonshire and Oxfordshire. A shortage of local youngsters is one of the reasons why many a village team folds. High property prices force them to live elsewhere and the second-home owners who can afford to buy are unlikely to plunge into the time-consuming business of village cricket on their weekends away with the family.

▲ Chacombe's original pavilion, perilously constructed out of packing cases, after its demolition by a falling horse chestnut tree.

This is not, though, a day for pondering about sociological change. It's a day for reminiscing about the fun and camaraderie shared during distant summers. We've strolled down the lane from the pub, turned right past the glorious array of autumnal trees around the manor house, and climbed over a metal gate into a somewhat rutted and muddy field. It's difficult to believe that it was hosting cricket just eight years ago. 'I reckon even I could get a bit of turn on this surface,' muses Alan Garrett, a batsman, who recently retired from the fire service at fifty.

From beyond the ditch we're being eyeballed by a herd of pale-faced Herefords. Roger has good reason to recall the days when sheep were kept there instead. 'Somebody launched one into the next county, probably off my bowling,' he remembers. 'We went looking for the ball only to find all these sheep lying on their backs with bloated stomachs. Luckily we had a shepherd in the team. Acker his name was. "They'll be all right, boy," he said. "Just stamp on their stomachs, but make sure it's towards the head end." So we had to leave the cricket for a while to deflate the flock. Acker was right. They just got up and walked away once we'd got rid of the sheep bloat.'

Hitting a six in the other direction, over the moat, could lead to confrontations with an even more unnerving form of animal life. Doberman Pinschers prowled the grounds. Still do, judging by a sign on a side gate in the lane. 'One of our team always had to go and get the ball back because we knew how to handle them,' Roger recalls. 'Whenever I drive past this place, I can't help think about the blood, sweat and tears that I expended on the pitch as it was then.' Bowling? 'No, rolling. We had a very heavy roller. Eventually we managed to acquire a diesel-powered road roller. Trouble was, though, it didn't have any brakes. You had to stall it when you reached the far end of the ground, then jump start it with a tractor.'

Back at the pub, the photographs are coming out. Here's one of Graham in his youth, smiting a ball to 'cow corner' under the scrutiny of an umpire with no trousers visible under his white coat. And here's another of the horse chestnut tree that blew down one night and demolished the original pavilion. 'I always knew those trees were a bit dodgy,' Graham maintains. Mind you, the pavilion was not exactly resilient. It was made of packing cases acquired from a Banbury factory. Its eventual replacement was a shed that had once housed battery hens. Didn't it smell a bit? 'Not once we'd cleaned it out,' puts in Graham's wife Sylvia. 'There was room for twenty-two men . . .'

'And ninety-eight chickens,' Graham murmurs.

She ignores him. 'And there was still space for us to make the teas.'

Here's yet another photo of poultry pecking around in front of that chicken- shed pavilion. They're geese apparently. Not chickens and certainly not ducks. Chacombe batsmen registered more than enough of the latter on that May day in 2002, shortly before its cricket team passed into history.

▼ Graham Watts smites a ball to cow corner at Chacombe. The umpire's trousers are most definitely short leg.

7: BRAMALL LANE

Bramall Lane, Sheffield, is a shrine to football. There is hardly anything to indicate that fewer than forty summers ago the home of Sheffield United FC was also a celebrated cricket ground. Apart, that is, from a plaque attached to one of the railings in the car park, pointing out that a Test match between England and Australia was played here in 1902.

Australia would come back on many more occasions as the century unfolded, but their opponents would be Yorkshire not England. They would play in front of large crowds, both voluble and knowledgeable, particularly before and just after the Second World War. Those were the days before Headingley had established itself as the official county headquarters. Sheffield rather than Leeds was where a peripatetic Yorkshire side felt most at home – certainly more at home than their opponents. Between 1919 and the final game in 1973, they played 163 championship matches at 'the Lane' and lost only 18. It was a place of 'sharp wit and shrewd comment', as J.M. Kilburn of the *Yorkshire Post* put it.

Kilburn was the Cardus of the east side of the Pennines. Born in Sheffield in 1909, he accepted Bramall Lane for what it was when he was growing up. Only gradually did he become aware of why visitors (particularly southern ones) might be less than enthusiastic about playing cricket in 'a pit of concrete and steel' with 'not a tree to be seen'. In *Homes of Cricket*, written with Norman Yardley in 1952, he describes not only the view from the pavilion but also the proximity of encircling industry: 'The clatter of passing tramcars and the scream of a saw-mill and factory hooters make a background of noise to the cricket, and a brewery chimney periodically pours smoke and soot into the air. An old story insists that the workmen in the brewery follow Yorkshire's fortunes with care, and stoke up most vigorously when Yorkshire's opponents are batting.'

◀◀ England's Wally Hammond drives a boundary off Cecil Pepper at Bramall Lane on 23 June 1945 on the first day of the match against Australia Services.

The brewery, Richdales (slogan: 'Richdales make rich ales'), is long gone. So, too, are the smoky skies and any sense that great cricketing deeds were once performed beneath them.

 A rare acknowledgement that cricket was played at Bramall Lane before football.

BRITAIN'S LOST
CRICKET GROUNDS

50

I am sitting in Bramall Lane's reception, under a photograph of the dauntingly corpulent former Sheffield United goalkeeper William 'Fatty' Foulke (1874–1916), waiting to meet the man who did more than anyone else to bring about an end to cricket on this ground. Robert Jackson is a spry octogenarian and a top crown green bowls player. He was once sports editor of Radio Sheffield and a long-time shareholder in Sheffield United Cricket and Football Club. Note which sport came first. Cricket was first played here in 1855; football not until 1889. The two coexisted until 1973, with one touchline running within twenty yards or so of the bowling crease. Not a recipe for a smooth outfield, particularly in the early season, as many visiting fielders would find to their cost when the ball reared up, evaded their grasp and sometimes sped on to the boundary.

'I reckon the other boundary would have been about here,' says Robert, sitting down under one of Fatty Foulke's tree-trunk legs. And the pavilion? 'That was out on the right-hand side of what's now the car park.' It was 'spacious and well-equipped,' according to Kilburn, 'though not very comfortable for watching the play. The home team have a very small balcony; the visitors have no balcony at all and must watch through glass, which is never very satisfactory.' Particularly, one imagines, if the windows were smeared with smoky residue.

There's not a trace of the pavilion today. Nor of the groundsman's house, which was roughly where two statues now stand: one to Derek Dooley, the other to Joe Shaw. Both former footballers, needless to say. Robert is a lover of cricket and football in season. So why did he push so hard to ensure that cricket would be banished from the Lane?

Coronation Pageant. Sheffield. M&S.21

'Because we had a three-sided football ground and I couldn't see United being successful as long as that remained the case. There was a much more attractive cricket ground at Abbeydale Park, Sheffield Collegiate's home turf, and Yorkshire went on to play there from 1974 until 1996.' Sheffield United CC, the club occupying Bramall Lane for the rest of the summer, moved out to Dore, the city's wealthiest suburb.

It was in 1971 that shareholders voted narrowly to accept Jackson's proposal to create a four-sided football ground. United were back in the old first division and doing well. But, as with any gathering of Yorkshire folk, there was no outbreak of universal harmony. 'One bloke told me: "Tha's got rid of cricket at Bramall Lane and I'm going to put a curse on the football team." I thought he was joking, but we've never achieved too much since.' Robert smiles wanly and leads the way round the front of the ground and in through an unlocked side gate. Red plastic seating encircles the pitch. Much of it would have been terracing at one time. Opposite the pavilion end was a long football stand raised above concrete terracing. 'Here the seating was slightly more comfortable than in the pavilion enclosure,' according to Kilburn, 'but the cricket was only distantly in view and a sense of isolation was discouragingly strong.'

As football gave way to the summer game, the Spion Kop was known as the Grinders' Stand. after the men who ground steel to make Sheffield cutlery. Sometimes they would go to a day's cricket after working a night shift in conditions that would make many of us long for nothing more than several pints of water (or Richdale's rich ales) and a long lie down.

Rudimentary wooden benches were provided, but Robert recalls that many of the stand's occupants preferred simply to squat on the edge of a terrace to pass judgment on the day's play. 'Anybody who ducked a bouncer was asked "What's tha' got a bat in thy hand for?" And there were no helmets in those days even if you were facing Fred Trueman.'

◄ A pageant at Bramall Lane for the Coronation of King George V in 1910.

◄◄ The spacious and well equipped pavilion at Bramall Lane, square on to the wicket with the belching brewery chimney behind it pictured in 1901.

Yorkshire v Lancashire at Bramall Lane in Sheffield on 1 August during the 1959
County Championship. Fred Trueman of Yorkshire delivers a bouncer to Geoff Pullar.

▶ Fred Trueman celebrates with a pint after a hard day's bowling for Yorkshire at Bramall Lane in 1968.

▼ The Australia Services team leave the pavilion to begin the day fielding at Bramall Lane.

Fred relished the support that he received from his fellow south Yorkshiremen at Bramall Lane. But he didn't get everything his own way. Tom Cartwright was still doing National Service when he played one of his first games for Warwickshire at Sheffield in 1955. He managed to battle his way to 27, but what he remembered above all was the belligerent attitude towards Trueman taken by eccentric umpire Alec Skelding. 'I can see Fred now,' Tom told his biographer, Stephen Chalke:

'He swore and cursed all through; he was appealing a lot and snatching his sweater. And Alec held on to it and yanked it back. "I'll clip his ear," he said to me. The crowd was getting more and more worked up. There was always this noise from the bank on the football stand side, and Alec said he was going to sort them out. I thought he was joking, but next moment he was over the fence. And there was this sudden hush. He came back and winked. "I told you I'd sort them out."'

It helped, no doubt, that Skelding had once been a heavyweight boxer who had fought Bombardier Billy Wells. Poor old John Warr of Middlesex could have done with Skelding's intimidating presence when he had a particularly miserable day at Bramall

Lane. He laboured long for no wickets whatsoever, was out for a duck and dropped a catch in front of the grinders. 'What's tha' coom oop here for, Warr?' boomed a voice from the terraces. 'To sharpen thy penknife?'

Middlesex was evidently not the most popular of counties in these parts. Denis Compton's capture of a stray dog on the boundary might have merited a round of applause. Instead there was uproarious laughter when the tyke – a Yorkshire terrier by all accounts – promptly bit him on the thumb. Compton was regarded as a dashing national treasure in much of England; here he was seen as a rival to Len Hutton.

But the crowd could give generous applause, even to a southerner, if they felt that he was playing exceedingly well.

▶ Two views of the packed crowd sitting in the bomb-damaged stands at Bramall Lane, for the first day of the England v Australia Services match at Bramall Lane in 1945. The pavilion can be seen in the bottom picture. A packed crowd at Bramall Lane was 'a place of sharp wit and shrewd comment,' according to J.M. Kilburn.

Kilburn recalled sitting in the Grinders' Stand in the 1920s when Maurice Tate of Sussex took the new ball for the last half-hour and bowled brilliantly with no luck whatsoever. 'He beat both Holmes and Sutcliffe and shaved the stumps; he had each batsman palpably missed by the wicketkeeper, who was playfully strangled at the end of the over. Tate's bowling was worth four wickets and he took none, but he was honoured by the "Grinders".'

A few years later, in the summer of 1933, the crowd rose as one and gave a tumultuous welcome to Douglas Jardine of Surrey, a southern 'toff' if ever there was one. Jardine, of course, had captained England to victory Down Under that winter in the controversial 'bodyline' series. Bramall Lane could be patriotic as well as partisan. The ground was still bomb-scarred in 1948 when the Australian tourists came to town and Sid Barnes was yorked by Yorkshire's Ron Aspinall in the first over to elicit a roar worthy of a winning

▲ Yorkshire's Geoff Boycott calls for a run as he hits out at Bramall Lane in a 1970 John Player League match. The slip fielder is Tom Cartwright.

▶ A rather less romantic prospect for cricket at Bramall Lane in 1960, as a gaunt and distinctly under-populated grandstand looks down on a Roses match between Yorkshire and Lancashire.

goal in the FA Cup final. And twenty years later, there were joyous scenes when Trueman led the county to a fabled victory over the Aussies by an innings and 69 runs.

By that time, however, the fight for a four-sided football ground was already under way and closure for cricket was just five years away. The last match was played between 4 and 7 August 1973. The scorecard carried an advert from the local paper offering the chance to 'win Bramall Lane cricket pitch and play in your front garden!' Fittingly, per-

▲ The modern football ground with cantilevered stands built on the cricket outfield that is Bramall Lane today.

haps, the opponents were Lancashire. Many an attritional battle between the trans-Pennine rivals had been fought out here. Only ten years previously, one G. Boycott had announced himself by becoming the first player to score a century on debut in a Roses match.

There was to be no repetition, alas. Boycott was out for 9 in a Yorkshire first innings of just 99. Lancashire didn't do much better. They were eight wickets down when they declared on 111 in search of a result after the Monday had been washed out by rain. Yorkshire's second innings started at 3 p.m. and by 5.30 they were 114 for 2 when Jack Simmons bowled the final ball to Colin Johnson, much to the frustration of a local resident who leaned out of his window and enquired plaintively: 'Dosta think I pay rent to live in Bramall Lane for *this*?'

It seems unlikely that he would have travelled out to Abbeydale Park to watch Yorkshire.

▲ Scorecard from the last game at Bramall Lane

8: SHILLINGLEE

At least the heavy roller is still there. To be precise, *a* heavy roller's still there. Rust-ridden as it is, it seems unlikely to be the same roller that ironed out the pitch on the Shillinglee estate when Prince Ranjitsinhji of Sussex and England installed himself at what briefly became his official residence on his return from India in 1907. That majestic batsman from the Golden Age had recently become the Jam Sahib of Nawanagar. The lack of much money to go with the title failed to deter him from embarking upon 'a Wodehousian summer of country-house cricket and creditors' summonses', as Simon Rae called it in his book on W.G. Grace.

Grace himself duly arrived with a team of twelve in May 1908, and, as Rae put it, 'threw himself into the spirit of Ranji's piratical extravaganza, posing in a turban in Shillinglee's extensive grounds and taking six wickets in the home team's first innings'. He failed with the bat, mind you, and 'gratified his host' by losing the match. The Jam Sahib could call upon a player of the calibre of Archie MacLaren, having summoned the Old Harrovian to Shillinglee as his private secretary, as well as some yeoman stalwarts from the Sussex side. Together they scored 599 against a Cambridge side captained by one N. Digby. Ranji contributed 103 in forty minutes and his XI duly won by an innings and 303. Later in that golden summer, however, MacLaren was summoned to appear before Guildford Magistrates' Court for non-payment of rates on Shillinglee. He paid up under protest.

It seems unlikely that he was reimbursed by the real culprit. Ranji simply carried on spending, fully aware no doubt that an Indian prince couldn't be prosecuted under UK law. Among his many creditors were a stationer in York and a wine merchant in Birmingham, who also supplied port and sherry to be shipped back to Nawanagar. His host, the sixth Earl of Winterton (who died only in 1962), had moved into one of the

◄◄ ▲ W.G. Grace's XI versus Ranjitsinhji's XI, 1908 – the teams posing outside the lodge. G.W. Beldam stands in the doorway wearing the thin-striped blazer, back row. A.C. Maclaren is immediately to the right of W.G. Grace.

◄◄ ▼ Ranji showing off his new motor car at Shillinglee in 1908. F.S. Jackson wears a moustache and hat in the doorway.

▲ Ranjitsinhji arrives at Shillinglee Park on 19 May 1908.

▶▶ ▼ Watching the cricket at Shillinglee Park in 1908.

▼ W.G. Grace (fourth right) with friends at Shillinglee Park, posing in Ranji's turban on 19 May, 1908.

estate outhouses to give the Jam Sahib and his retinue free run of the family's Palladian 'pile'. Ranji left owing £100 10s 2d in rent to the man who would later become Paymaster General as well as president of Sussex.

In his memoirs, the sixth Earl suggested that he was a better cricketer than his father, who had played twelve times for the county. His grandfather turned out twice for Sussex, albeit with a 22-year gap in between his two appearances, and once top scored for the MCC while playing against the county. 'In 1847, he was facing the bowling of Fred Caesar (brother of the celebrated Julius) in the Godalming versus Shillinglee match when a sparrow was killed by the ball he was due to receive,' says writer Roger Packham, who knows a thing or two about country house cricket in this neck of the woods.

It was the fourth and fifth Earls who had the pitch laid out in the first place, here between the Sussex Downs and the Surrey Hills. Shillinglee is just about in West Sussex, although the nearest village, Chiddingfold, is across the Surrey border. Local villages and towns provided not only the opposition but also quite a few team members. The estate's gardener, David Heather, was a regular and in 1855 he helped to bowl out the Surrey Militia for a grand total of 0.

Quite how long cricket continued after Ranji's departure is open to debate. Not even the diligent researchers of the Chiddingfold Archive can tell us precisely. All we know is that the house was badly damaged by a fire while occupied by the First Canadian Army Division in 1943. (The sixth Earl didn't have much luck with guests.) The building remained derelict until 1976, when it was bought by a developer and converted into apartments. In the meantime, the old cricket ground was turned into a nine-hole golf course.

No golf here now. A few horses from a nearby equestrian centre graze on the ground that played host to Grace, C.B. Fry, MacLaren and the incomparable if impecunious Ranji. Not to mention the brother of Julius Caesar.

Watching the cricket at Shillinglee in 1908. The moustachioed gentleman with his pads on is Lord Hawke.

9: BASS

The Derbyshire writer and historian Roy Christian described the Bass ground in Burton as 'anchored somewhere in no man's land, apparently in mid-stream'. I can see what he means as we leave a busy bridge over the Trent and judder down a pot-holed track into a low-lying area that seems to be encircled by the river. At the far end is the Burton Cricket Club, founded by Abraham Bass in 1827 and still thriving. Would that the same could be said about the adjoining ground that once proudly bore the Bass family name, evolving into Bass-Worthington in 1927.

I'm being chauffeured by Burton chairman Pete Pritchard, who stops half way down the track, opens a five-bar gate and drives his 4 x 4 on to land that's now run by a syndicate known as the Washlands Sports Club. They offer crown green bowls, tennis, fishing and football. No cricket, however, since around the end of the twentieth century. 'Cricket is labour-intensive,' Pete observes, lighting up another of his favourite Hamlet cigars. 'The days when most breweries were prepared to pay for full-time groundsmen to work all week to prepare a wicket for a match on a Saturday have long gone.'

Abraham Bass was part of a brewing dynasty. He was also known as 'the father of Midland cricket', turning out for Nottinghamshire a few times, representing the North against the MCC at Lord's, playing in an All England XI and putting his much-admired batting technique at the disposal of the Gentlemen of Staffordshire. It seems likely that he laid out this ground as well as Burton CC's, which is further down the rutted track. But he died in 1882, two years after the brewery team hosted its first match. Through the trees behind the pavilion we can still see the former maltings of what was once a brewery renowned throughout the British Empire.

'The pitch was square on to the pavilion,' Pete recalls. 'That was the Burton end,' he adds, waving the Hamlet back in the direction of the bridge, 'and that was the Newton end, after a village called Newton Solney.' The pavilion itself has a vaguely half-timbered appearance as though somebody had started to build a mock Tudor pub and run out of wood.

'There was always generous hospitality when you came here,' says Derbyshire county statistician David Duffieldbank. No shortage of after-match Bass or Worthington E, in other words. Now seventy-eight, he played fifty seasons in club cricket as a wicket-keeper-batsman and finally hung up his pads eight years ago. 'The last match I played at Bass was for a team called the Grasshoppers in 1992–3,' he continues. 'There was a howling gale and we had to abandon any hope of the bails staying on for long.'

The county second XI used what later became known as the Bass-Worthington ground for ten seasons until 1987, but the first team visited only twice: in the scorching summers of 1975 and '76. Oxford University one year, Cambridge the next. 'That Oxford match was my last first-class game,' Harold Rhodes recalls. 'I'd finished in 1969 and was playing club cricket, but the county must have been a bit short that day and asked me if I'd turn out.' Derbyshire won by 81 runs. Not before one Vic Marks had hit 98 in the second innings, batting at number three. The only notable score in Oxford's first innings was 54 from another promising youngster called Imran Khan.

'After the Cambridge game the following summer, it was decided that the pitch wasn't suitable for first-class cricket,' Duffieldbank confides. And it certainly wouldn't be fit for cricket of any kind now unless a very heavy roller was taken to that rutted football pitch. 'Time to move on,' says Pete as a chilly gust blows in from the Trent, scattering brittle brown leaves across the studded mud.

10: WENTWORTH WOODHOUSE

William Henry Lawrence Peter Wentworth-Fitzwilliam not only had a very long name; he also inherited an extremely large property. At 606ft, the eastern front of Wentworth Woodhouse remains the longest country house façade in Europe. Plenty of windows to aim at. But Peter, the name the eighth Earl Fitzwilliam finally settled on, knew he was on safe ground when he offered a fiver to any cricketer who could break one with a six. A Botham, a Hammond or a Jessop might struggle.

'It was the biggest pitch I ever played on and it was hard enough to hit a four,' says long-term Wentworth opening batsman Ernie Laister. Not that he, personally, had too many opportunities. He was fourteen in 1949 when the last official match was played here in this stunning relic of feudal south Yorkshire. Peter Fitzwilliam had died the previous year when a private aeroplane carrying himself and John Kennedy's sister Kathleen crashed into a French mountainside. His former home was about to be turned into Lady Mabel College of physical education and, beyond the cricket pitch, the largest open-cast mine in the country was steadily consuming substantial chunks of landscaped parkland on the orders of Manny Shinwell, Minister of Fuel and Power.

'I remember us playing on those Coal Board lorries when we were kids,' Ernie says. 'But I was delivering newspapers to the house when I was first roped in to play cricket. Wentworth must have been a man short because they asked me to field. And I must have done all right because, after the match, the captain asked me if I wanted to go to nets the following Monday.'

The team was made up of estate workers and a few miners. The viscounts and majors who had stayed at the house and sometimes played during the 1920s and '30s were rarities during those pinched post-war years. 'I sometimes wish I'd been a bit older,' Ernie reflects. 'The Wentworth team was well looked after. They went all over the place in the estate's lorry, all expenses paid apart from their beer money, and the social life was fantastic by all accounts.'

◀◀ ▲ The Wentworth Woodhouse cricket team of 1934, posing outside the magnificent East Front of the house.

◀◀ ▼ Viscount Milton's XI v Yorkshire Gentlemen at Wentworth Woodhouse, 1 September 1924. Viscount Milton is second from left in the front row.

There was no pavilion for home games. Apart from those visiting viscounts and majors, players changed in the fives court and took tea in the servants' hall. 'There were about 750 estate workers at one time,' puts in Wentworth Cricket Club's vice-chairman Martyn Johnson, 'and around fifty pits within a ten-mile radius, most of them with well-maintained grounds.'

A singular character is Martyn, a retired Sheffield bobby who recently wrote his memoirs under the title *What's Tha Up To*. Now sixty-nine, he once faced the young Freddie Trueman while playing for his native Darfield. 'You just put your bat out and hoped for the best,' he shrugs as we sit in the George and Dragon, just round the corner from his home, one of the now soot-free stone cottages that the Fitzwilliams built for their workers. 'Good cricketers always had first option on a house in the village,' he confides, and Ernie concurs. 'My opening partner, Norman Birley, was a steel worker, but he got a house here because he could play a bit.'

Ernie's family moved to the village when he was three. He worked as a carpenter and joiner, initially for the estate, and carried on playing until well into his seventies. The Wentworth village team now plays its home games behind the nearby Rockingham Arms, named after the first Marquess of Rockingham (1693–1750) who began the building of Wentworth Woodhouse. His former house is now occupied, in part, by an architect and the grounds have long since been re-landscaped. There are plenty of pheasants out there, but no cricket players, even in high summer.

▼ The vast east frontage of Wentworth Woodhouse. The cricket ground was directly in front, but far enough away for any would-be six-hitter to struggle to break a window.

One of many nostalgic photographs on the walls of the George and Dragon shows the team as it was in 1934 with the big house just about visible in the background. Ernie points out Tom Gale, the gamekeeper, his daughter Helen Gale, who served the team as scorer, and William Oates, who went on to play for Yorkshire. 'And there's the keeper, Frank Sylvester, who once told me a story about a fast bowler – Blagborough I think his name was – who had a very long run-up. He disappeared towards Betty Gill's end—'

'Nobody knows who she was,' interjects Martyn, 'but the pond was named after her.'

Ernie resumes the story: 'Anyway, the visiting batsmen shouted to Frank: "If yon bowler goes back any further, he'll need a bike." Blagborough came steaming in, knocked out his middle stump and, as usual, followed through so far that he was up at the wicket by the time he'd come to a halt. When Frank told him what had been said, he shouted after the batsman: "Tha's the one who needs the bike now."'

Well, it was a long walk back to the boundary.

Ernie was to play one more match on that enormous pitch in the late 1950s. 'Lady Maud Fitzwilliam had gone to live in Malton,' he explains, 'and it was arranged that their village team should come down and play us in front of what had been her old house. Trouble is that the original pitch had grown over and the groundsman had to lay a new one sharpish. It turned out to be a shocker. What was supposed to be a full day, eleven to six, ended very early with a lot of low scores.'

The windows were never remotely threatened.

11: LLANILAR

As the name suggests, the Showfield was not primarily a cricket ground. It belonged to a local landowner from the Castle Hill Estate in Ceredigion who staged an agricultural show on the site every August. The Llanilar village team was expected to arrange away fixtures on those occasions, leaving the square roped off to protect it. But then the possibility of that prized stretch of turf still being trampled upon by several tons of prime Welsh Black bull was one of the trade-offs that cricketers accepted in return for being allowed to play in one of the most stunning settings in Wales and, indeed, anywhere in the UK. Never mind that the outfield was largely devoid of grass in the early part of the season because one of several local flocks had been grazing there since lambing time.

The pitch was laid across a comparatively gentle slope – for these parts anyway. Much steeper hills reared up beyond the chapel, church and pub that bordered the boundary. It was a reasonably good batting track, according to Robin Varley, a Mancunian geography teacher and deputy head who came here from nearby Aberystwyth University in 1974 when the club was just getting under way. 'We didn't have a ground at the time, so we hired a pitch from the university,' he recalls. 'But it was a time when a lot of keen cricketers were emerging in the neighbourhood and we needed a home of our own. Eventually we did a grace-and-favour deal with the estate.'

The first significant game was played on a bone-hard pitch in the hot, dry summer of 1976. 'We were playing on a new square that had formerly been at the middle of a football pitch,' Robin goes on. 'And we didn't possess a heavy roller.' A bit lively then? 'It was. And our opponents were St Fagan's from Cardiff, a very useful side that would go on to win the National Village Knockout Competition at Lord's a few years later. Well, this competition had to be played on a Sunday. Bang went our tacit agreement with the chapel. So we did a deal that we'd start early so that chapel-goers mounting the steps at

◀◀ Alan Jones of Glamorgan calls at the start of his benefit match at Llanilar in 1980. Tossing is Robin Varley of the home side.

◀◀ Cars parked around the showfield for the county's visit.

▶ Alan Jones goes in to open the Glamorgan batting with John Hopkins.

six p.m. wouldn't be affronted by the sight of cricket being played on the Sabbath. As it turned out, St Fagan's bowled us out for 39 and the match was all over by three.'

Llanilar fared better as the pitch settled down. In 1978 they saw off two top sides from the first division of the South Wales Cricket Association – Pontarddulais and Gowerton from Swansea. 'They [Gowerton] found themselves changing in a former classroom (desks and chairs designed for nine-year-olds) in the community centre, 50 yards or so from the ground which they entered via a pub car park,' Robin writes in his book *The History of Cricket in Aberystwyth*:

▲ The Glamorgan team of 1980 at Llanilar.

'Once on the ground, their scorer would have been invited to join ours, Tom Parry Edwards, on a bench set before a rickety table which had once adorned Frank Keyse's kitchen. While practising before the game, they could not help but be taken in by the dreamy rural atmosphere of this beautiful field, behind a pub, in the middle of a small village complete with medieval church tower, nestling in a deep river valley. Who wouldn't relax under such circumstances?'

The author scored 103 for Llanilar, including five sixes and five fours, out of a total of 171 for 9 in forty overs. Enter John Shaw, that rare breed among cricketers: a fast-bowling social worker. In a previous match he had taken 8 for 6. On this occasion, thundering in from the chapel end, he helped bowl out Gowerton for 150. Heady days indeed and hearty after-match celebrations in the Falcon after the match. The pub did even brisker business in 1980 when the Showfield hosted a Glamorgan XI for Alan Jones's benefit year. Having been edged to the boundary a couple of times, the future West Indian fast bowler Ezra Moseley sent down a few bouncers. 'It was fortunate for the Llanilar batsmen that the pitch was fairly soft following heavy rain before the game,' Robin ruefully records, going on to add: 'The field looked a picture, with marquees, deck chairs and plenty of spectators.' Glamorgan won at a stroll and Alan Jones pocketed £400, considered a good sum at the time.

Two years later, the landowner fell ill and the Castle Hill Estate passed into the hands of her children. The new trustees allowed two houses to be built at the bottom of the field. Gardens were bordered with barbed wire. Assurances were sought that there would be no damage to property from flying balls. 'We were supposed to provide absolute indemnity,' Robin recalls, 'and they wouldn't accept that our insurance provided perfectly adequate cover.' Result: stalemate. Llanilar upped stumps and moved back down the road to Aberystwyth. But not before winning the West Wales Cricket Club Conference league with a stirring victory over their nearest rivals, Llandovery.

Free champagne flowed in the Falcon that night. The new landlord must have thought he had fallen on his feet as the drink (and the money) flowed. Little did he know – nor indeed did anyone else present on that joyful occasion – that the Showfield had hosted its last game of cricket.

▼ John James of Llanilar sees his leg stump knocked back in 1981.

Anthony Evans and Robin Varley (wearing blue cap) stride out to bat for Llanilar.

12: CIRENCESTER

Former Gloucestershire chairman John Light cut his cricketing teeth at Cirencester Grammar School in the late 1950s – forty years on from the arrival there of one of the finest players England has ever produced. 'I remember scoring 50 not out in my second game for the first XI and walking past two old codgers on the pavilion steps,' says Light. '"Well done, young John," said one of them. "But you'll never be as good as Walter."' Few were.

Walter Reginald Hammond arrived from Portsmouth as a boarder in 1918, aged fifteen. He spent the next two years giving the school's scorer writer's cramp as he rewrote the record books. In house matches alone he hit 614 in four innings, including one of 365 not out. For the first XI his average was 57.84. His top score was 110 not out and his bowling figures were even more impressive – 25 wickets for 50 runs in 32 overs, giving him an average of 2. 'People forget that he could bowl as well as play football,' says former detective sergeant Ralph Wilkins, another Old Grammarian. 'Wally also turned out for Bristol Rovers.'

His head teacher, Tom Frazer, revelled in having such a gifted ball-player at the school's disposal. Along with everyone else, he must have gaped with astonishment as this callow youth deposited yet another six over the banks of the River Churn. Hammond was the son of a serving soldier in need of a father figure and the cricket-mad Frazer was happy to oblige. 'He was Wally's mentor,' Ralph assures me, going on to disclose that the head's ashes were scattered over the school wicket at a dawn ceremony in 1945.

He'd be turning in his grave if he knew that no cricket has been played there for over forty years. The grammar school merged with two secondary moderns in 1966, forming a new comprehensive on the edge of town. A primary school now occupies the site and perhaps we should be grateful for small mercies. At a time when government is once again trying to slash budgets for school sports and developers hover like

◀◀ ▲ The Old Boys' annual gathering at Cirencester Grammar School in 1930: The Headmaster greets and shakes hands with Walter Hammond.

◀◀ ▼ An aerial view of Cirencester Grammar School, showing the edge of the cricket field in the top left of the picture.

 Parents' Day, June 1953: the exciting cricket match between the parents and the school that was eventually won at 7 p.m. by the parents.

vultures, there's still a playing field behind the old building. The wicket, ashes and all, has been trampled on by generations of growing feet.

Grammar school old boys are left with their memories. John Light would have been in his mid-teens in 1955 when Gloucestershire came to play the Old Grammarians for wicketkeeper Andy Wilson's benefit season. 'Our head teacher closed the school at 2 p.m. so we could sit round the boundary to augment the sparse ground,' he recalls. 'I think the game only raised thirty quid. There would have been far more there if Tom Graveney had turned out. But he was playing for England at

the time and this was his one day off. "I hadn't the heart to ask him," Andy said later.'

And did the county win?

'They'd have won it if they'd all been forced to bowl left handed from the town end. Or the railway end, for that matter.' Thanks to Dr Beeching, trains stopped running over the embankment shortly before the grammar school went comprehensive. The handsome pavilion has long gone too. 'It must have been in a pretty rotten state after a while,' adds John. 'Probably went on the town bonfire. It was always held on the school field.'

At least there's now some official recognition of the great cricketing feats that were once performed here. The Old Grammarians recently affixed a blue plaque to the Victorian building that still houses part of the current school. 'Walter Reginald Hammond: 1903–65,' it reads. 'World renowned cricketer, Walter Hammond, captain of England and Gloucestershire County Cricket Club, was a pupil at this school, then Cirencester Grammar School, from 1918–1920.'

There wouldn't be room for his batting and bowling figures.

▲ The 1951 School First XI in front of the pavilion. The team had a poor season, winning only 3 matches and losing 8.

◀◀ ▲ The combined Old Boys and School cricket teams of Cirencester Grammar School at the 1931 fixture, posed in front of the pavilion. Wally Hammond is in the centre, front row. The two innings match was completed in one day between 12 o'clock and 7, and won by the Old Boys, with Hammond caught and bowled for a duck in the first innings and top-scoring with 63 in the second.

13: HOFFMANN

County cricket has never been much of a money-spinner. But there has to be a bottom line, as the accountants would put it. Mr Micawber would have put it more like this: 'Expenditure £697 one shilling and ninepence, income £725 5s 9d; result happiness. Expenditure £841 8s 3d, income £501 7s 3d; result?' Well, not exactly misery, but a bit of a headache for whoever had to balance the books for Essex CCC in 1961, ten years before the advent of decimal currency. (Note to younger readers: a shilling was worth 5p and 3d was just over 1p.)

The income and expenditure accounts above relate to first-class matches played at the sports ground owned by Hoffmann's, which had been Britain's first manufacturer of ball bearings when it opened for business in Chelmsford in 1898. Essex played Lancashire there in August, 1959, and 5,554 turned up over three days, ensuring a profit of £97 13s 10d. For one reason or another, attendances were sparser when Hoffmann's staged a Cricket Week in June 1961. A County Championship match against Derbyshire was followed by a game against the South African Fezelas. Surprisingly, perhaps, the Fezelas proved far less of a pull, attracting only just over 501 spectators in three days. This for a team that included Eddie Barlow, Roy McLean, Colin Bland and Peter Pollock.

'They were all young and comparatively unknown at the time and I think the public didn't go for what was seen as a friendly against the youth or second team,' Tony Debenham surmises. Tony is the chairman of the Museum and Library Committee at Essex and his car is nosing through foggy suburban thoroughfares in search of the

▲ A rapt crowd packed in to Hoffmann's ground to watch Essex play Lancashire in 1961.

ground owned by the company that would eventually evolve into Ransome Hoffmann Pollard. Ransome made lawnmowers, which seems somehow appropriate for cricket sponsors. But it was Hoffmann's ball bearing factory that built the wealth thanks to which much of Chelmsford's sporting and social life flourished. The company not only employed well over 7,000 people at one time; it also paid for a nationally renowned brass band, a male-voice choir and what was considered the finest sprung dance floor in East Anglia. Not to mention an eight-acre field made suitable for all outdoor sports, including cricket.

Only the bowls club remains. 'There it is,' says a voice from the back seat of Tony's car. Robin Hobbs, the last English leg spinner to take over 1,000 wickets in his first-class career, is pointing through the fog at a vague shape at the end of a short drive. On closer inspection it turns out to be a sizeable wooden structure. Robin stands with his back to the club headquarters and peers across the car park. What would have been the bowling green end where he twirled away nearly fifty summers ago is now covered by the garden of a late '80s semi. The semi itself stands roughly where the pavilion would have been. Hoffmann's paid for a new, prefabricated pavilion in 1964. 'It was quite a substantial building,' Robin remembers. Far more so than the old Nissen hut that was still standing, just about, near one of the sight screens. In the distance we can see the tops of mature trees that would have provided a pleasant backdrop to the ground's far end. 'They were always there,' he confirms.

But he doesn't feel particularly nostalgic about Hoffmann's Sports and Social Club Ground. It was one of many that the itinerant Essex team played on in those days. 'That Derbyshire game was one of my first,' he reflects. 'And all I can remember about it was using my foot to try to stop a ball. It rolled over my boot and went on to the boundary. Ken Preston, the senior pro, came out from slip and gave me a right roasting.' As punishment, perhaps, the nineteen-year-old was never given the chance to bowl. To cap it all, he was out for a duck in his only innings in a drawn match, and then dropped for the Fezelas game. 'Yes, I managed to avoid that one,' he adds with a wry smile. 'My fellow leg spinner Bill Greensmith was hit for five sixes in one over by Denis Lindsay.'

Another, rather better-known Denis rolled into town four years later. Denis Compton came out of retirement to play for the International Cavaliers at the Hoffmann ground. Three years shy of his fiftieth birthday, he was caught Pritchard bowled Hobbs for 30. Robin has to be reminded by Tony that he took 4 for 55 in that game. Another victim was Trevor Bailey. Never renowned for his cavalier batting, we can only assume that the Essex and England stalwart all-rounder had switched sides to make up the numbers.

The following year Essex settled into their current home at the County Ground, a mile or so across town from where we're standing. But they did return to Hoffmann's one more time for a John Player League game in 1969. 'We spent a long time in that pavilion,' Robin recalls, 'because it rained most of the day.' Only five overs were possible. Essex had made 37 for 1 when the match was abandoned.

By the early 1980s, the works team was being abandoned as an all-too-familiar scenario unfolded. The ground staff was halved from two to one and, in 1984, even the turf was rolled up and sold off on the company's orders. Three years later, the Department of the Environment finally gave permission for housing to be built on the site, and by the end of the decade, what was now known as the RHP Group had moved to Newark in Nottinghamshire. British manufacturing had to become 'leaner and fitter', to use the terminology of the times.

There was a need to increase income and cut expenditure. Happiness had nothing to do with it.

14: THE CIRCLE

Mike Ulyatt pulls up in the car park of Hull City's KC Stadium and tries to get his bearings. 'See those trees,' he says, pointing at two rare deviations from the horizontal in an expanse of tarmac. 'The Hull Brewery tent was just beyond them.' It was known as 'Critics' Corner' when the Anlaby Road cricket ground, otherwise known as The Circle, was in its pomp. Yorkshire crowds have never been shy of voicing their opinions, and as the beer went down so the volume went up in the days when the county team made regular treks 'out east'. Crowds of around 8,000 would turn out to watch the side, Mike among them.

The only surprise is that he didn't *play* here for Hull CC, having had a trial for Yorkshire when he was fourteen in 1954, alongside another locally born youngster, Jimmy Binks. While Binks went on to keep wicket for a very successful county side, Mike would become business advertising manager for the *Hull Daily Mail*, turning out regularly for Hull Railway Clerks. 'Our ground was next door to The Circle, right where we're parked now,' he says. Indeed it was used for overflow parking during county matches.

Yorkshire coming to town was a big event, judging by Mike's book *See You Down at The Circle*, which is full of pictures, stories and statistics. On page 29, for instance, we learn that Ray Illingworth hit his maiden century here, 146 not out, against Essex in 1953. Three years later he took 6 for 15 against Scotland. When I rang Illingworth to remind him of those feats, he was well aware of the figures but in no mood for warm reminiscences. 'All I remember about playing in Hull,' he said, 'was that the ground was wide open, it was bloody cold and smelt of fish.'

It seems that Illy may not have been alone in failing to relish going to Hull and back. 'I think some of the Yorkshire lads would have been happier to stay in Leeds,' Mike muses. 'I asked Michael Vaughan about it once and he said "Hull? It was always

◀◀ Geoff Boycott and Martin Moxon prepare to open the batting at The Circle in Boycott's joint benefit match with Ian Botham in July, 1984.

▲ Yorkshire v Kent at The Circle, Hull in the County Championship on 16 June 1955. Len Hutton of Yorkshire plays a shot.

windy out there."' Perhaps he should think himself lucky. By Vaughan's time there was far less chance of the wind whiffing of fish – a sign that it was going to rain, according to the locals – and, anyway, The Circle's days were numbered.

The ground would have looked far better in Len Hutton's day, when the handsome late Victorian pavilion was still standing. Yet Hutton once complained: 'The constant stoppages for steam trains going in and out of the nearby Paragon Station behind the bowler's arm was a big distraction to me.' Still, the trains didn't stop Hutton, on his twenty-first birthday, putting on 315 for the first wicket against Leicestershire with Herbert Sutcliffe in 1937. One of the Leicestershire bowlers was heard to mutter: 'I'd rather be back working down the pit than bowling to these two buggers.'

Brian Close was better disposed towards Hull, praising the wicket and the crowd. But then it was at The Circle that he captained Yorkshire to victory over Surrey to win their third County Championship on the trot in 1968. He fielded at short leg to put pressure on the visitors and one fierce shot on to his shin rebounded into the gloves of the redoubtable Binks. Seemingly impervious to pain, Close played on despite the blood seeping through his flannels. He was only persuaded to go to hospital for a tetanus jab once the trophy was secured. 'When I got back, the lads had finished all the champagne,' he grumbled.

Memories, memories. It's time to get out of the car and locate where the wicket was. Mike leads the way into the stadium, where two Johns are waiting for us. John

Mowbray, who first played cricket here in 1950, is a hale and hearty eighty-eight and still a director of Hull CC; John Cooper is operations manager here at the KC. We're hot on his heels as he sets off through a warren of corridors until we emerge into the players' tunnel. 'This is about where the pavilion was,' says John Mowbray. 'It was a wonderful building, but it was in the wrong place. By two in the afternoon it was freezing because the sun was behind us. Also it was square on to the wicket.' And where was the wicket? 'In what's now the centre circle.'

So the main square of The Circle was inside the centre circle and square on to the pavilion. Got that? Good.

Around us are the banks of plastic seating of a modern football ground that has already hosted a season of Premier League football as well as gigs by Elton John and The Who. But it evidently rankles with Mr Mowbray that, apart from The Circle Restaurant, there is nothing to indicate that this was once the principal cricket ground in East Yorkshire.

It opened for business in 1898 on a perfect circle of land, 180 yards in diameter, replacing Hull CC's former ground in Argyle Street, which was required for expansion by the North Eastern Railway Company. Most of the land round here was owned by the railway and it was on the company's insistence that the pavilion, built mostly of wood and painted dark green, should face east. Members must have felt those chill and fishy winds even more than the players, who at least had the benefit of being able to

▼ The Circle ground on 1 August 1974.

The F.S. Trueman International XI poses in front of The Circle's impressive pavilion with members of the opposing team, a Humberside XI. In the back row can be seen Peter Lever, Don Wilson, Phil Sharpe, David Steele, Frank Hayes, John Edrich and Alan Ward. In the front row we can see Tom Graveney, Fred Trueman, Ray Illingworth and Bob Taylor.

▲ The Circle ground on 1 August 1974. The tallest man is Peter Lovell, local fish merchant, cricketer with Hull Zingari CC and one-time president of Hull Cricket Club.

run around. Yet Hull cricket thrived in this setting during the 1920s and '30s, attracting big crowds for club matches and even bigger ones for the county's bi-annual visits.

The club was even more successful in the immediate post-war years, winning Yorkshire League Championships every season bar two from 1947 until 1953. That was the year when a bungalow for the groundsman was built on the far side from the pavilion. It was to prove a mixed blessing for future inhabitants. When Wally Hillaby took over the post from George Cawthray in 1969, they sat outside the bungalow, having a drink together and watching a county match. Suddenly the ball whizzed past them and thudded into the door. George was apparently unperturbed. 'You'll have to get used to that, Wally,' he told his successor. 'I was once sat in the lounge having a glass of beer when a ball came straight through the window and smashed my glass. Spoilt my beer it did.'

Five years later Yorkshire played their last County Championship game at The Circle. It was a benefit match for Geoff Boycott, but it was Worcestershire's Basil D'Oliveira who stole the show with a superb 227. The county continued to travel to Hull for Sunday league games into the 1990s. But by that time the writing was on the wall. To be more precise, the writing was on ambitious plans for a new football stadium.

'The rot started when the pavilion was condemned as unfit in 1986 and demolished the following year,' says Mike. 'It was replaced by portable units for the changing room, but The Circle had lost the feel of a proper cricket ground.'

Wally Hillaby and his wife moved out of the groundsman's bungalow and vandalism increased. Drained of resources, the club eventually accepted an offer of £250,000 to vacate their ground and make way for the future. The future of Anlaby Road belonged to Hull City. Hull Cricket Club played their last game at Anlaby Road in September 2000. A decade later and The Circle Restaurant is all that the KC Stadium has to show for just over a century of cricketing memories.

Apart, that is, from two trees that once formed the portal to Critics' Corner.

▼ Hull City FC's KC Stadium, built on the site of The Circle.

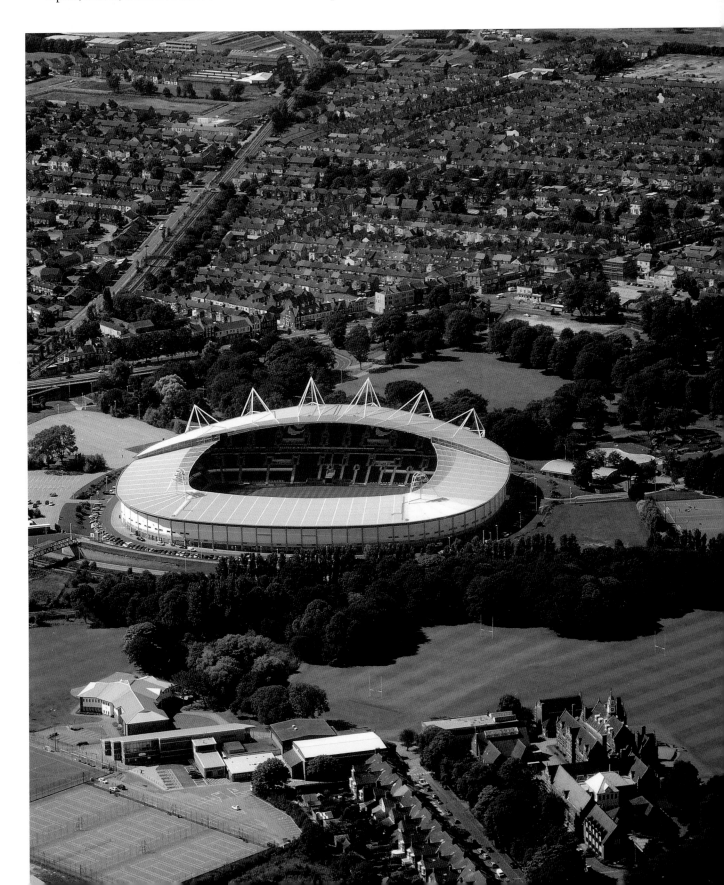

15: ROYAL ARSENAL CO-OPERATIVE

The imposing half-timbered pavilion at the Royal Arsenal Co-Operative Society Cricket Club, since burnt down by vandals.

There are green fields as far as the eye can see. Which wouldn't be so surprising were we not in south-east London. Admittedly, we're in New Eltham not New Cross, and this is green belt land. Flat land, as it happens, broken up by mature trees and scrubby hedgerows. Litter-pickers in bright orange jackets are resignedly plucking lager cans out of the undergrowth.

Each patch of ground across this great green swathe contains a playing field marked out with a football pitch or five. That's what you might expect in the middle of February. Come April, at one time, there would have been a transition. As the trees came into bud, the goal posts and corner flags would have come down and the heavy roller been dragged out. Not any longer. Not at the former Unilever ground, the former Old Shootershillians (Grammar School) ground, nor the former Hays Wharf ground – the latter a legacy of the days when London had docks rather than Docklands. Not at the one-time home of the Royal Arsenal Co-operative Society Cricket Club either.

We're standing somewhere between the edge of a penalty area and the centre circle on well-studded mud while Mike Donnelly points out the site of the old RACS square. 'There were twenty-five wickets on that,' he says. 'The first team track went that-a-way,' he adds, pointing to distant metal railings beyond which a red double-decker is passing by. 'That was the Footscray Road end and the other way was the Unilever end. It's now Charlton's training ground.' As a season-ticket holder at,The Valley, home of Charlton Athletic FC, Mike can't really complain about that. But as a cricket lover he admits to 'a sense of melancholy' when he recalls so many enjoyable summer weekends wielding the willow or tossing up his leg breaks on the pitches now occupied by Eltham Town FC's Youth Academy.

'It was a very good wicket for batting,' he assures me, and he ought to know. Now seventy-three, he first played for the Co-op at the age of fifteen when he started work there as a clerk. Apart from a brief break for National Service, he carried on playing for them until he was sixty-four. For over two-thirds of that time he held down a place in the first team, which makes his career figures particularly impressive. He scored more than 52,000 runs, including fifty-five centuries, at an average of 50 plus. Those leg breaks were pretty useful too, accounting for over 1,600 wickets at an average of 13. Admittedly, the last four years of his career were played at the Metrogas Sports Ground, home to RACS since they were obliged to leave Footscray Road in 1998. So how did that come about?

'Well, the Royal Arsenal became part of the Co-operative Wholesale Society and they obviously realised that they were paying out a lot to keep this place going. There were two full-time groundsmen as well as bar staff and people employed to make the teas. Apart from cricket and football, tennis, bowls and squash were played here and there was quite a social scene with a bar and a dance floor inside the pavilion.'

The pavilion itself was an imposing half-timbered structure, with a slate roof in which was embedded a large clock. All that remains of it are the steps next to the old squash courts. 'Not long after we moved out,' Mike continues, 'the vandals got in and burnt the place down. Then the grass started growing. It was knee-high at one time. The CWS was keen to accept a £2 million offer to build a leisure centre here, but Greenwich Council wouldn't give planning permission because it's part of the green belt.'

That grass was finally hacked down when Eltham Town, the club that fostered the talents of future England captain Rio Ferdinand, moved its academy to the site two years ago. A useful footballer in his day, Mike has no problem with youngsters exercising their lungs and developing their ball skills. But he wouldn't be human if he didn't look back longingly at some of the golden summers of his own youth. RACS eventually graduated to the very competitive Kent League and he remembers, back in the 1960s, opening the batting for the Association of Kent Cricket Clubs against a Kent second team that included Alan Knott, Derek Underwood and Mike Denness. 'I got 29 and scored a few off Underwood,' he recalls. 'But it was Norman Graham who gave us the most problems. He was six foot eight and everything lifted. You were playing off your chest most of the time.'

Watching from the boundary that day was one Colin Cowdrey. 'And he stayed for a drink afterwards. I can see my dad standing proudly at the bar with him,' Mike smiles. The accountants – even Co-operative ones – can force you to take your bat and ball elsewhere, but they can't take away your memories.

▼ The wicket at the RACS ground in New Eltham was always good for batting.

ROYAL ARSENAL
CO-OPERATIVE

91

16: STAVELEY

But for the factory at one end, it would be the perfect village ground, overlooked on two sides by the voluptuous green foothills of the Lake District. Opposite the pavilion end was the river – the River Kent, to be precise, flowing down from those hills en route to Morecambe Bay. 'You spent half your time fishing the ball out of the water when Keith Donoghue was playing for Staveley,' says John Glaister, who turned out for Warton and wrote a book on the Westmorland Cricket League called *Of Smittle Spots and Sticky Buns*. A 'smittle' is Cumbrian dialect for 'a catching area' apparently. And Donoghue? Well, he was known locally as 'The Don', which speaks for itself.

It was his batting and Phil Nicholson's formidable fast bowling down the slope from the factory end that helped Staveley, the south Lakeland village halfway between Kendal and Windermere, now home to the burgeoning Hawkshead Brewery, to win the First Division of what was briefly known as the South Lakeland League in 1987. Their pitch, laid out before the war on ground that had formerly been a rubbish tip, was not conducive to easy batting, unless you had the talent of The Don. Visitors approached it with some trepidation, especially when Phil had ball in hand. Frank Monks remembers nursing a broken finger in the pub one evening after keeping to Phil. 'There were no sight screens,' John Glaister recalls, 'and the ball was either subterranean or hitting you in the mouth.' As a bowler himself, though, he relished the conditions. 'I never got fewer than five wickets there.'

Back in 1966, Staveley won all three trophies open to them: the Vaux Tankard, the John Thexton Trophy, and the First Division. Former club president Harry Lewthwaite, now 87, remembers it as though it was yesterday. In fact, he can recall the club's performances all the way back to 1934. On his living-room wall he has a beautiful water-

◀◀ Twenty years after the last game of cricket, the groundsman's mower is all too conspicuous by its absence at the former Staveley CC's Back Lane ground. Happier times, with the mower preparing the outfield for the next match, are evoked by Don Mounsey's idyllic watercolour of the same view when the ground was in its heyday.

colour of the ground in its bucolic heyday: green wooden pavilion, the hills light with sun, and the groundsman mowing the turf ready for the next match.

These days, sadly, a mower is most conspicuous by its absence. Four years after their triumph in the old South Lakeland League, Staveley were ejected from their Back Lane ground, and the padlocked field is now knee-high in buttercups and dock leaves. The neighbouring factory's construction had annexed a sizeable portion of what had previously been 'quite a big ground', according to Harry Lewthwaite — 'three and a half acres'. Twenty years after its expansion plans stopped play, the factory is closed. 'They wanted to build on it back in 1991, but couldn't get permission because we're in a national park,' explains Frank Monks. Now the land is apparently up for sale. Frustrating? 'Just a bit. Half the lads in the team worked at the factory and every time they had a brew [tea break], they were looking out over the place where they played.'

Like Frank, master batsman Keith Donoghue still lives in the village, having 'married a Staveley lass' and set up home 'right there,' he says, pointing to the top window of the end-of-terrace house overlooking the ground. And like Frank, he walks past the ground every day and feels the same sentiment. 'What a waste,' they both say at different times. 'There's nothing for the youngsters now, apart from football on the rec.' They both said that as well. But where does the club play now? Nowhere, says Frank. It came to an end when the ground did.

The Don is still turning out for nearby Kendal's third team at seventy-three. Three years ago he was presented with a Lifetime Achiever award by Cumbria Cricket Board. Harry Lewthwaite is emphatic: 'He was the greatest batsman in the Westmorland League'. 'I don't know what all the fuss is about,' Keith said at the time. 'I just love playing cricket.' He shrugs off those sixes into the river: 'It didn't happen that often; usually it bounced back off the trees.' But sometimes it soared over them and the river itself, I'm told. 'Well, it was a small ground,' says Keith. A small boy had to be despatched to a bridge half a mile away. By the time he'd retrieved the ball and returned with it, he must have covered the best part of two miles, which at least gave the bowler a lengthy breather.

Staveley's pavilion was what Frank calls 'a typical Westmorland League job: small and wooden with a changing room either side of a little kitchen. The wives and girl-friends used to make the teas until the eighties when there was a bit of a rebellion.' Feminism had evidently reached Cumbria by that time. 'Well, they were saying things like "I get enough of this at home". So we went to the Duke William for our tea instead. The landlord was very considerate. He'd put on soup if it was a four-sweater day and sandwiches with cakes if it was reasonably warm outside.'

These days the ground is more nature reserve than cricket field, but at least it's still there. 'It would have to be completely re-seeded,' muses Harry Lewthwaite. 'What we need is a benefactor', reflects Frank as he and Keith lean on the gate contemplating the riot of vegetation. Burneside down the road, he explains, found someone to buy them a new ground. Where is the John Paul Getty of the Lake District who can take Staveley back to Back Lane?

▲ The Staveley Cricket Club team of 1987: South Lakeland League Division One Champions. Frank Monks is third from left in the back row, Keith Donoghue second left in the front row, Phil Nicholson in front with the bat.

17: NEWSTEAD

At one time you only had to whistle down a pit shaft, as the old cliché had it, to bring up a fast bowler. Aptly enough for those in the business of hewing coal, they tended to be fiery characters. Nonetheless, an opposition batsman at Newstead Colliery must have been somewhat taken aback to see one of the home team's speed merchants hurtling in from what was known as the 'top end' with smoke billowing from his backside.

Dave Atkins was his name and, like quite a few of his team-mates back in the 1960s, he would have done a Saturday morning shift down the pit before embarking on five hours of cricket. 'He liked a couple of pints before the match to lay the dust,' recalls long-term wicketkeeper Mike Murphy, still stumping at sixty-seven, and chairman of what is now Newstead Abbey and Village Cricket Club in the South Notts League. 'Dave also liked a cigarette and he had a habit of lighting up when he was fielding on the boundary, well away from our captain Billy "Goat Gruff" Radford. Somehow he didn't notice that the tip of his fag had come in contact with the rag that he kept in his back pocket to polish the ball. It was smouldering nicely by the time he came in to bowl. Luckily, we managed to put it out before too much damage was caused.'

The damage done to mining communities by wholesale pit closures in the 1980s has never been rectified. Here in the heart of what was once Sherwood Forest, little landscaped patches of colliery waste are crested by mock winding wheels marking the spot below which men worked in dirty, difficult and sometimes dangerous conditions. There's one just up the road at Annesley, where Joe Hardstaff junior started work as a

▲ The Newstead Colliery cricket team in the 1950s.

pit pony minder when he was fourteen. Twelve years previously, his father, namesake and cricketing mentor 'Old' Joe had moved the family to 25 Fishers Street, Nuncargate, next door but two to the Larwoods.

'Harold and Joe would have played here at one time or another. Bill Voce too,' Mike reflects as we park next door to a bowling green, the last remnant of a once-thriving miners' welfare at Newstead. The colliery was closed down in 1987 and cricket ceased soon after. From the front of Mike's 4 x 4, we can see the backs of the new houses that were built on the old ground. 'That's where the pavilion was,' he says, pointing to a rather soulless semi-detached. 'Lovely half-timbered 1930s building it was.'

Hot showers were, apparently, provided by coal-fired electricity. 'Afterwards we'd all pile into the welfare and drink with the opposition. They usually stayed on in those days. The bar used to open for the evening session at six and we'd play till about eight. For two hours or so, men would come out with their pints and stand round the boundary to watch. There was a concrete edge around the perimeter, and beyond that were the allotments. If the ball went over there, you almost always had to find a new one.' Particularly, it would seem, towards the end of the summer when a worn red sphere could be completely hidden under the shadow of marrows the size of zeppelins and onions that could prick the tear ducts from twenty yards. Miners grew vegetables with the competitive edge that they brought to whippet-breeding and cricket.

Mike never worked down the pit. He was a clerk in the local Coal Board office when he started playing here in 1960, aged fifteen. Keeping wicket on the old Newstead Colliery pitch required a youthful athleticism. 'Every pit had its own groundsman, supplied by the Coal Industry Social Welfare Organisation [CISWO], and this one was hard and true,' he recalls. 'But we had some lively bowlers and there was a slight slope. Luckily, Howard Burrows preferred to bowl uphill from the welfare end. He was very tall and brought the ball down from well over nine feet.'

The cricket was not quite so competitive by the 1980s, Mike maintains. But the colliery team was still producing useful players when closure came. Five or six of them joined Newstead Abbey and helped propel the club up the league. What was once Lord Byron's stately pile is just down the road from the former pit village and the grounds provide an idyllic backdrop for cricket. 'It *is* lovely,' Mike concedes, 'particularly in early summer when the rhododendrons are out. But the pitch is too small for first-team cricket in this league and we can't do much about it – or rebuild the pavilion – because of the restrictions on a heritage site.'

So while he and his second-team colleagues press on in this sylvan setting, the first team now plays on a new ground across the railway line, laid down by the local borough council. 'I think they wanted to put some life back into the area,' Mike surmises as we pull up next to one of those mock winding wheels commemorating Newstead Colliery (1884–1987). He leaves the heater on. It's deep mid-winter and the pitch is currently hosting football. But we can see the covers in the shadow of a small factory making reinforced concrete and providing what looks like one of the few means of employment round here. 'The setting's pretty bland,' he sighs, 'and the pitch is nowhere near as good as the old one. Anything we leave outside gets vandalised. Even the heavy roller.'

▲ A view of the former Miners' Welfare from the site of the cricket ground at Newstead Colliery, now mostly covered with houses.

18: SOUTHAMPTON

'No Ball Games', proclaims a notice attached to a wall of honeyed stone in a rather upmarket Southampton housing estate. One or two letters are missing but the message is clear. What is missing altogether is any sense of irony. No ball games indeed! This area was once the ball-playing hub of the city. Southampton FC's old home, The Dell, was close by and Hampshire's former County Ground is buried somewhere under these meandering cul-de-sacs of neo-Georgian town houses with pillared portals, their driveways occupied by expensive cars.

At least the existence of that cradle of cricket, known locally as Northlands Road, from 1885 to 2000 is acknowledged by a handsome plaque, sited on the corner of one of several thoroughfares named after cricketers who graced the ground. Marshall Square, for example. But would that be Roy Marshall or Malcolm Marshall? Both played here with distinction, Roy for nineteen summers and Malcolm for thirteen. The great West Indian fast bowler – terrifying to face but charming face to face, by all accounts – coached here as well, until shortly before his untimely death from cancer in 1999.

Today I'm with Roy Marshall's former opening partner, Jimmy Gray, now in his mid-eighties. His blue BMW pulls up outside Greenidge Court. Almost as soon as we climb out, he points between the new houses and apartments to a rather different sort of property dating back to at least the 1960s. 'Geoff Keith had a place there with a flat roof and his missus was fond of nude sunbathing,' he recalls. 'The boys used to keep an eye out for her.' Between overs, of course.

Today is not a day for sunbathing. In fact, it's bitterly cold as we slither across icy pavements to a point near a snowman that looks as though it has partially melted and then re-frozen. It squats impassively, like a diminutive umpire, while Jimmy gets his bearings. 'The nets would have been alongside this fence,' he says. 'We used to have to do some coaching here at Easter time every new season, and it always seemed almost

◀◀ The devastating opening partnership of Gordon Greenidge and Barry Richards striding out to open the batting for Hampshire at Northlands Road in Southampton in the 1970s when spectators were allowed on the pitch at lunch and tea. They took their time to leave the field.

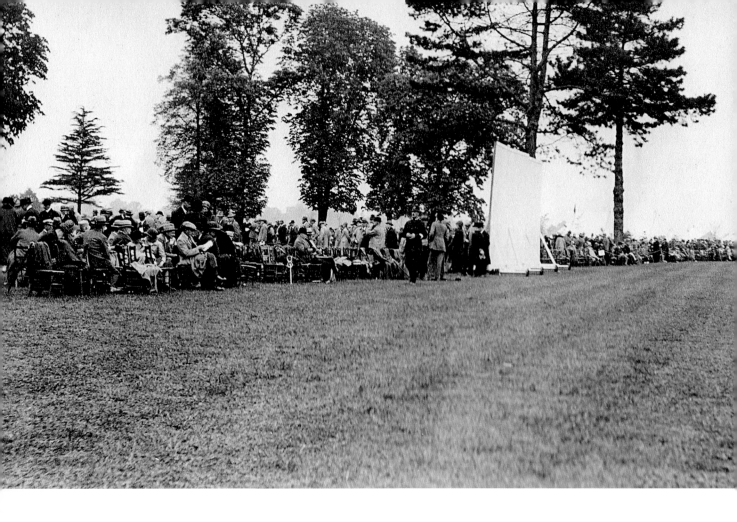

as cold as it is now. Oh yes, and the indoor school was over there.' And the pavilion?
'That was a lovely old building. There was a men's stand and a ladies' stand at one
time, and I remember catching Graeme Pollock out once, right in front of the men's.'
Well, you would, wouldn't you? Probably glad to see the back of him.

What about the other side of the ground, Jimmy? 'That was known as the stadium
end because there was a speedway track and an ice rink there.' And which did you pre-
fer with ball in hand? 'Didn't bother me. As long as I was in the team, I was happy.'

This county stalwart knew his place in the scheme of things. He also knew every
blade of grass on the pitch. Like many another apprentice who started here after the
war, he had to help pull an extremely heavy roller across it between nine and ten each
morning. 'One of those horse-drawn jobs it was, and we were the horses,' he chuckles,
before conceding that it was good for building up the strength and stamina required by
a pace bowler like himself.

When it came to opening the batting with the first team, he knew that his job was to
keep his end up while Roy Marshall blazed a trail. 'I had the best view in the ground
when Roy was in full flow,' he smiles. But let's not forget that J.R. Gray scored more
runs for Hampshire than any Southampton-born player, passing 2,000 in a season on
three occasions, and hitting 213 not out against Derbyshire in 1962. What's more, he
took over 400 wickets, including a career–best 7 for 52 against Glamorgan at Swansea in
1955.

When I suggest that there should be a Gray Lane among the cricketing closes, crofts
and courts hereabouts, he laughs dryly and looks at me as though to say: 'You must be
joking.' And perhaps he has a point. Hampshire now has, in the Rose Bowl, an arena tai-
lor-made for Test cricket. In the past, however, it never seemed to have much trouble

attracting top players to the more homely confines of Northlands Road. Apart from the two Marshalls, there were Barry Richards and Gordon Greenidge – a formidable opening partnership if ever there was one. David Gower and Robin Smith played under Mark Nicholas's captaincy in the 1990s. (All were outshone in 1996 when Kevan James took four wickets in four balls against India here – Tendulkar's and Dravid's among them – before following up with a century.) And then there was Phil Mead, the left-hander who bestrode the old County Ground like a Colossus. You'd have to be getting on a bit to remember him, mind you. From 1905 to 1936 he made 138 centuries in 700 matches, more than any other Hampshire player before or since.

Jimmy's happiest memories of Northlands Road revolve around Colin Ingleby-Mackenzie. Not surprisingly, perhaps, because it was under the captaincy of that buccaneering Old Etonian that Hampshire won their first County Championship in 1961. 'Colin was the best social mixer I've ever known,' he says as we climb back into the BMW. 'He did a bit of work as a rep for Guinness and he always had a boot full of bottles to celebrate our victories.' As well, presumably, as Ingleby-Mackenzie's wins on the gee-gees. He used to ask umpires at the County Ground to keep a radio about their person after lunch so that he could check on the racing results.

'He was a fantastic man and sorely missed,' affirms Peter Sainsbury, Jimmy's golfing partner and former county colleague in those heady days of the early '60s. Peter was still around in 1973 when Hampshire won the title again. He, too, was an all-rounder, batting right-handed while bowling with his left. Did he, by any chance, have a favourite end?

'Not really. There was only one end available and that was the one that Shack didn't fancy. The rest of us were quite happy to take the other one.' But then Derek Shackleton *was* one of the most effective exponents of line and length that any captain could have at his disposal.

Like Jimmy Gray, Peter knew his place in the scheme of things at Northlands Road. As young pros in the 1950s, part of their job was to bowl to members in the nets. 'Somebody batting in a cravat might balance four bob [20p] on one of the stumps and

▼ Three of the greatest players of Hampshire in the modern era, all in action at Northlands Road: left to right: Barry Richards Malcolm Marshall Robin Smith

▲ A full house at Northlands Road looks out over a parched outfield during a Nat West one-day game in 1999.

tell you it was yours if you could knock it off,' Peter recalls. 'We were only on about a fiver a week in those days.' The challenge was taken up with relish and, more often than not, successfully accomplished. Young Sainsbury was no mean player after all. A regular for twenty-two seasons, he became the first man to take seven wickets in a one-day match when he claimed 7 for 30 against Norfolk in the first round of the Gillette Cup, 1965. In 1974, he was named one of Wisden's Five Cricketers of the Year.

'I'd relive every second of my career again if I could,' he says wistfully. If he was playing for Hampshire today, I remind him, it would be at the Rose Bowl. The impressive new venue opened for business in May 2001. Only just over seven months earlier, the final County Championship match against Yorkshire at Northlands Road had provided rich entertainment for an emotional crowd, with sixteen wickets falling on the first day. Day three was rained off and Hampshire eventually lost in the final over. They were relegated and about to say goodbye to their old ground. But that didn't stop the inspectors (led by Mike Denness) fining them eight points for the state of the pitch. Two days later there was a Sunday league game against Nottinghamshire. Hampshire lost that one, too. A bugler played the Last Post and the flag was lowered over the pavilion. Shane Warne signed and dated the match ball (a white one) and handed it to the club historian, Dave Allen.

He still has it, along with the match stumps and a piece of turf acquired at an auction of memorabilia from the 7.68 acre site, staged shortly before the bulldozers moved in. The spirit of John Arlott, Hampshire born and bred, would have been looking down on the occasion. Back in 1958, he wrote in the *Cricket Journal*: 'The Southampton ground has an air of improvisation, of gradual growth, additions and afterthoughts merging into a unity like the photos, nick-nacks and pieces of china which, over the years, accumulated on our grandparents' mantelpieces.'

Nearly thirty years on and more hard-headed officials were already looking for a new ground. Editor Andrew Renshaw explained why in an article for the *Hampshire Handbook* entitled 'The Road to the Rose Bowl (1987–2001)': 'Members and spectators had known for years that the buildings and the facilities, from the car park to the toilets, were not suitable for a sporting venue: acceptable for ordinary days of county cricket, perhaps, when the spectators just outnumbered the stewards, but not for the more popular days on the cricket calendar such as tourist matches, one-day semifinals and World Cup games.'

The capacity, after all, was around 4,500 compared to the Rose Bowl's 20,000. Having finally secured a National Lottery grant of £7,176,728 in August 1996, Hampshire CCC sold the old County Ground to Berkeley Homes on 25 February

End of an era:

 The Hampshire team come out on the balcony after the final game against Yorkshire in 2000. Robin Smith leads the way, followed by Shane Warne.

▼ The crowd says its final farewell to the hallowed turf.

1998. It would have been Arlott's eighty-fourth birthday. The sale brought in another £5,735,000. But grant and major housing deal added together still don't buy you a Test ground on a prime site in southern England, and the county walked something of a financial tightrope before it was able to unveil the Rose Bowl in all its splendour. The summer of 2011 saw Hampshire host its first Test match, when England entertained Sri Lanka. There was also a one-day international against India in September. Australia and Pakistan had played there in one-day games against England the previous season.

What do the old pros think of the new ground, I ask Messrs Sainsbury and Gray.

'I had a super day up there with some of the old players,' says Peter. 'It's a wonderful stadium, but we were right at the back of a stand and my eyesight's not what it was.

The pitch seemed an awfully long way away. At Northlands Road you felt as though you knew most of the spectators.'

Jimmy felt that too. 'The crowd always felt really close to you when you were out there,' he reflects over a warming cup of tea back at his house. He remembers one day in particular when the spectators seemed closer than ever. The West Indies came to Hampshire on a high in July 1950, having just beaten England for the first time – at Lord's, what's more. 'Cricket, lovely cricket' would become a calypso anthem. No wonder the crowds were clamouring to see them at Northlands Road. 'They kept moving the rope in to accommodate more and more people sitting in the outfield,' Jimmy recalls. Perhaps the shortness of the boundary helps to explain how Everton Weekes, coming in just after lunch, hit 246 not out before close of play.

Forty-four years later, Dave Allen found himself in a small bar in Barbados. He fell into conversation with four elderly locals who broke off from playing cards to talk about cricket. One of them was very knowledgeable indeed about that innings in 1950. Surely it wasn't the great man himself? 'No doubt about it,' says Dave. 'He remembered going for his 250 with the last ball and being denied the four when the ball smashed into the stumps at the other end and stopped dead. All this started when he casually asked me where I came from and the County Ground, Southampton, inevitably found its way into the conversation. "Ah, yes," he said. "I know the place."'

You wouldn't know it now, Sir Everton. You wouldn't know it now.

The County ground in the context of its surroundings.

19: HINCKLEY

▲ County cricket at
Hinckley in August 1911
between Leicestershire v
Warwickshire. Note the
sight screen: a sheet.

The itinerant Essex side of the 1950s and early '60s seemed to like the ground at
Coventry Road in Hinckley. Leicestershire secretary Mike Turner would receive a letter
before the fixtures for the season were finalised, asking if they could play there. Why
should that be so? Was it that they didn't fancy the county ground at Grace Road in
nearby Leicester, or was there another reason? Turner suspects the latter. 'Hinckley was
well known for the manufacture of ladies' stockings and, on cricket week, the hosiery
manufacturers were very generous.'

It seems unlikely that transvestism was rife in the Essex dressing room, so perhaps
we can assume that taking home a pair of silky 15-denier was a good way of pleasing
wives and girlfriends. County cricketers are away from home a lot and anything that
kept the missus happy must have been all right by them. Still fresh in collective memory was the American GI cutting a swathe through British womanhood with offers of
sheer nylons and tins of pineapple chunks.

Mike himself played at Hinckley only for Leicestershire's second team. He became
better known as an administrator than as a player and is credited with being the pioneer of one-day county cricket in this country. That form of the game, however, was
still in its infancy when his county's first team played the last of its seventeen games
here in 1964. Each match had required a considerable upheaval to move the focus
from Grace Road to Coventry Road.

'All the seats had to be transported from Leicester in three removal lorries,' Mike
recalls. 'We also had to bring a mobile scoreboard and all the marquees.' He was sitting
in the secretary's tent one day when he had a surprise intrusion from Stanley
Jayasinghe, whom he'd recently signed from Sri Lanka – or Ceylon as it was known at
the time. 'Stanley was on his way out to the wicket from the pavilion when he made a
detour, poked his head around the tent flap and said: "I'll get you a fifty today." He was

a pro but he batted Corinthian-style and scored just 50 on a difficult wicket. On the way back, he made a detour again and said: "I told you so."'

At least the county team didn't have to transport a pavilion to Hinckley. One had already been built there with breezeblocks fronted by concrete and topped by a corrugated iron roof. 'There were two communal baths and two lengthy changing rooms,' says John Coe, chairman of Hinckley Town CC, as his 4 x 4 edges through the rush-hour traffic on Coventry Road. 'And that's roughly where it was,' he assures me after we've parked and sidled down a passageway by what is now a vet's surgery. All we can see beyond a large, spreading conifer and a garden fence is the back of a house built some time in the 1970s. It was towards the end of that decade that the Hinckley club accepted an offer from a local developer and moved to a much bigger site at Leicester Road on the edge of town, where the county side – David Gower and Jonathan Agnew among them – returned to play in the 1980s. As a builder, John was charged with putting up a clubhouse that overlooks the cricket pitch one way and rugby fields the other.

In his days as a player at Coventry Road, the rugby and cricket players shared the same ground at different times. 'It meant that the outfield was a nightmare in the early part of the season,' he goes on. As a lad in the late 1940s, he'd played on Hinckley's first ground at nearby Ashby Road shortly before it, too, disappeared under housing. 'Facilities there were much more primitive,' he recalls. 'The sight screens were old bed sheets.'

Coventry Road must have seemed positively palatial by comparison. The county side made its first appearance there in 1951, but it was the match four years later that sticks in John's mind. Brian Statham finished with figures of 6 for 20 as Lancashire shot out the home side for just 42. Leicestershire did better in the second innings. Not much better, however. They were all out for 81 and lost by an innings and 101 runs.

It would be fair to say that this was not the county side's most fruitful out ground. They were dismissed for under 100 on six occasions. And six of their seventeen games here were against neighbouring Warwickshire. Big-hitting Jim Stewart made 182 not out in a second-wicket partnership of 223 with Khalid (Billy) Ibadulla when Warwick romped home by eight wickets in 1962.

Captaining the visitors that day was Mike (M.J.K.) Smith, who took six catches in Leicestershire's second innings. He was the son of one of those Hinckley hosiery magnates. 'They pushed the boat out for visiting teams because, for them, it was usually a once-a-year affair,' he recalls. Having waited all season for a county side to visit, there were times when two came along at once. Before Warwickshire in June 1962, Essex had breezed into town. They too won by eight wickets before pocketing their stockings and heading south.

▼ The Coventry Road ground at Hinckley with its corrugated-iron-roofed pavilion.

THE CRICKET GROUND
AND
PAVILION

situated in the South Park a few yards from the entrance to the Station Approach and extending to an area of about

5 a. 2 r. 29 p.
(5·680 acres)

The Cricket Ground

measures about 470 feet by 400 feet and is rectangular in shape. It is practically dead level all over and has been frequently used until recently for minor County Matches.
The Bletchley Town Club have been temporarily granted the use of the Ground and Pavilion, rent free.

The Modern Pavilion

situated in the centre of the south-east boundary is a well-designed structure of brick with a tiled roof and consists of a centre portion and two wings. Along the front is a Verandah which opens into the main apartment measuring 64 feet by 20 feet with leaded windows along the entire north-west side, all of which can be opened. Folding partitions at each end enclose Two Dressing rooms, each of which has a separate entrance from the Playing Field, and Cloakrooms at the rear include

Two lavatory basins and W.C.'s.

Staircases at each end of the Verandah lead up to A BALCONY, both ends of which are covered. At the back of the Pavilion are Kitchen, fitted sink and dresser, Wash-up place with copper and Serving room, and in a Small Yard are Stoke Hole and Coal Shed.
Main Drainage, Companies' Water and Electric light are installed.

In the north-west corner of the Ground, shaded by trees, is a TIMBER-BUILT SCORING BOX. and the Ground is enclosed on three sides by continuous iron railings.

The main entrance from the road is through

A Pair of Ornamental Wrought Iron Gates

hung on brick and carved stone pillars and guarded by

AN ATTRACTIVE LODGE

built of brick with a tiled roof partly tile-hung and timbered, and rough-cast. It contains a tiled Hall with Staircase ; Front room ; Kitchenette with concrete floor, fitted sink and range ; Larder, and Three Bedrooms above. Outside wash-house and W.C. Main Drainage is connected and Companies' Water and Electric Light are laid on.

The Lodge is occupied by a service tenant, but subject to this occupation,

VACANT POSSESSION OF THIS LOT WILL BE GIVEN ON COMPLETION OF THE PURCHASE.

20: BLETCHLEY PARK

The boffins based at Bletchley Park during the Second World War worked around the clock in their ultimately successful quest to break German codes and save thousands of lives as a result. But did the code breakers ever take a break and, if so, how did they relax? Cricket, perhaps? A cerebral game, for sure, and they happened to have on their doorstep what had been one of the finest grounds in Buckinghamshire, overlooked by a majestic pavilion.

Cerebral it may be, but cricket is also time-consuming and the code breakers' lunch break was not extensive. So, on warm summer days some of them played a form of rounders. Well, once the Wrens moved in, women outnumbered men by three to one. There were quite a few Americans there as well. So what emerged eventually was a combination of rounders and baseball. Dons devised and decreed the rules. In Latin. They played with a tennis ball and a sawn-off broomstick on the croquet lawn in front of the vastly imposing Victorian mansion that had been the home of the Leon family until 1938.

Sir Herbert Leon, Liberal MP, local benefactor and cricket lover, had died twelve years previously. He left £700,000 in his will at a time when the average wage was £2 a week. But he had been a financier who had made a pile on the stock market. Indeed one of the earliest games on his private ground was between a Leon Bros XI and the Stock Exchange Staff. The exact date and the scores are rather difficult to establish from a report in the local paper because the correspondent seemed more inclined to tell his readers about the fine weather and that 'everybody was hospitably entertained by Lady Leon at lunch and tea.'

Her name was Fanny and she was Sir Herbert's second wife. After his death, she became president of the new Bletchley Town Cricket Club which played its home games here until the early 1950s when they moved to a new ground at nearby Manor Fields. Club president Tony Clarke, still keeping wicket for the third team at 75, remembers playing for the Boys' Brigade against the Bletchley team in the late 1940s. Soon he was co-opted into the Town team and, at seventeen, he took over from his father, Jim, behind the stumps.

◄◄ A page from the sale catalogue for the Bletchley Park Estate from 1938.

Jim Clarke had been a legendary figure on the local cricketing circuit. He played originally for Woolstone where the family farm was sited before it was compulsorily purchased to prepare the way for the new town of Milton Keynes. In 1933 he had smashed 175 for the village team in 75 minutes, including 21 sixes. Bletchley Park, used on occasions for Buckinghamshire's minor county games, must have been altogether grander than Woolstone's ground, I suggest. 'It was,' says Tony. 'But Dad still used to hit 'em over that big tree in the corner of the ground.'

Not even Clarke senior, though, managed to break a window in one of the huts built to accommodate the Wrens during the war. 'They were a fair way from the pitch,' says his son, 'but there seemed to be a hell of a lot of them.' One of his other early memories is of steam and smoke wafting across from nearby Bletchley Station. Not enough, mind you, to obscure his view of the ball and a very fine piece of turf.

It must have made quite an impression on the young Tony Clarke as he would go on to make a career out of laying down cricket squares all over the country. So what was the one at Bletchley like? 'Good and true. There was a football pitch at one end and the pavilion at the other.' And what a pavilion! A classic example of elaborate late-nineteenth-century architecture, it was used as the local Liberal Party headquarters as they campaigned for Sir Herbert Leon at election time. So what was it like inside, Tony? 'A bit like the one that the Rothschilds built at Ascott Park – lots of wood panelling.'

▼ A sylvan prospect of the Bletchley Park ground, and its splendidly gabled pavilion, framed by the 'big tree' over which Jim Clarke used to hit sixes.

◀ The magnificent late-19th century pavilion left to rot on a patch of wasteland.

The pavilion is still standing. Just about. When Bletchley Town moved out, to make way for a proposed further-education college, the Park ground was used for a while by the local grammar school. 'I remember playing there for the masters against the boys,' says former history teacher Robin Bowen-Williams, now 69. 'One of the older lads was genuinely fast and able to make it lift. Let's say he was aiming more for the body than the stumps.' 'Twas ever thus in such matches: a chance to seek what pupils regarded as revenge. But the grammar school eventually merged with a local secondary modern to form a new comprehensive with its own playing fields. Cricket at Bletchley Park was effectively over. The pavilion briefly became the headquarters of a music college before being completely abandoned.

What remains is now fenced off from the Bletchley campus of Milton Keynes College, under which there is a cricket pitch somewhere. The pavilion has apparently been left to rot on a patch of wasteland bordered by two main roads. 'I find this incredibly sad,' says Kelsey Griffin, director of museum operations at Bletchley Park, as we trudge up a muddy track at the back of the college and observe the ruin at close quarters. The rotting wood of the veranda and the pavilion steps are almost completely obscured by brambles and wintry wisps of rose bay willow herb. Windows are either missing or boarded up. A weather cock sits precariously atop a be-domed and decorative miniature tower just about clinging to a sloping roof with many missing tiles and clumps of moss gathered in the eaves. There are even fewer roof tiles round the back of the building, but a red-brick chimney worthy of Lutyens juts defiantly skyward.

'You wouldn't want to see inside,' Robin assures me later. Probably not. But I would like to know who owns it. Turns out to be a company called Maltmore Ltd. At least that was the case in May, 2010 when Milton Keynes Council last did a land registry search. A quick search online suggests that there is no longer a development company of that name. Injunctions have had to be served on previous owners to halt damage to the building by falling trees. 'It [the pavilion] is on our Heritage at Risk Register as one of our more urgent cases,' said a Council spokesman, 'although our powers are limited because it's not listed.'

More's the pity. Who knows? If those wartime boffins had played cricket instead of rounders, a very fine piece of sporting architecture might have been saved for the nation. Then again, perhaps it's just as well that they took short lunch breaks. Were it not for the code-breakers working extremely long hours, we might not have had a nation to save it for.

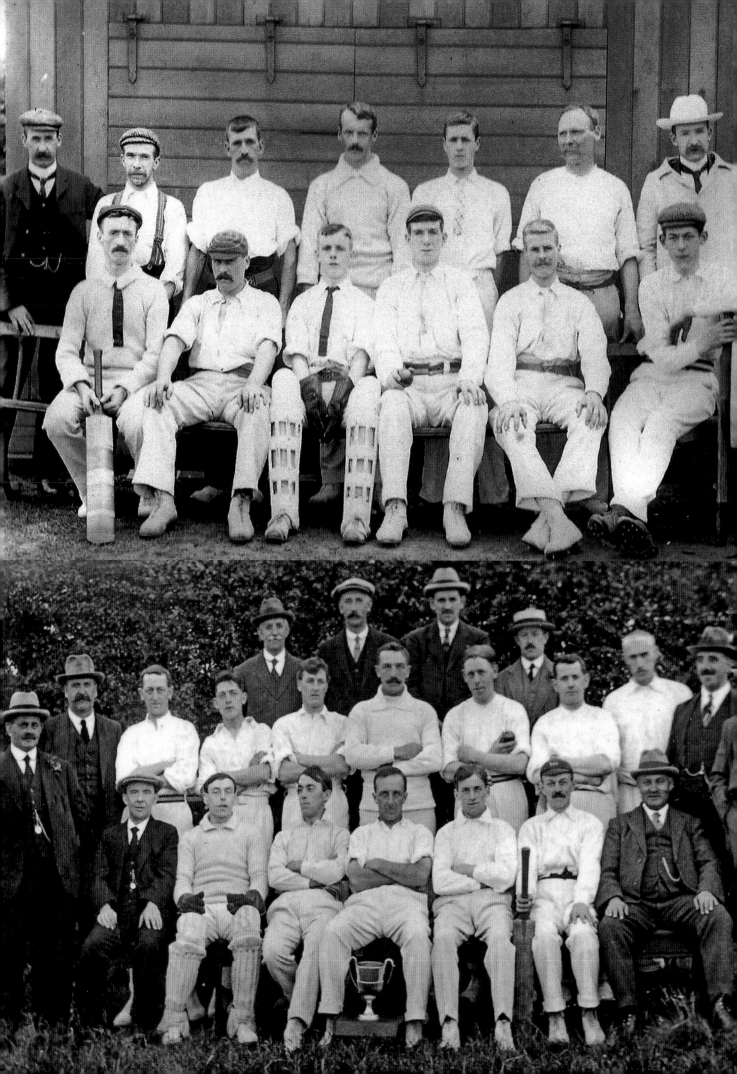

21: SKELMERSDALE

Inevitably perhaps, a tone of regret is threaded through this book. Cricket-lovers and former players look back at the Elysian fields of their youth – fields that have since been buried under shopping centres, turned over to other sports or simply abandoned by social and economic forces beyond their control. But sometimes change is for the better. When I ask Alan Forster about Skelmersdale CC's decision in 1998 to move from its old School Lane ground, his only regret is that his seventy summers and a dodgy knee preclude him from playing on the new ground.

'Once you see it, you're just itching to bat on it,' he assures me. I'm going to see it for myself in half an hour or so. For now we stand looking at the site where Alan gave stalwart service to 'Skem', as the town is known locally, for over thirty-five years. We're just off School Lane in a cul-de-sac of modern two- and three-bedroom houses called Headingley Close. Yes, *Headingley*, and, yes, we're in Lancashire. Who dreamed that one up? The developers, presumably. Well, at least they made the local cricket club an offer it couldn't refuse. Officials used the money to pay a company run by former Lancashire and England bowler Peter Lever to lay out the new ground on the edge of town. School Lane and Headingley Close are now part of a development known as The Willows.

There's no wind in The Willows this morning. It's a sharp, clear and sunny winter's day, and the swings in the children's playground hang empty and still. Somewhere near them were the creases where Alan used to take guard to face whatever was coming at him from either the duck pond end or the tennis courts end – former West Indies Test all-rounder Collis King on one occasion. 'He was playing for Westoughton by that time and he'd shortened his run-up,' Alan recalls. 'Just as well. Ours wasn't the biggest

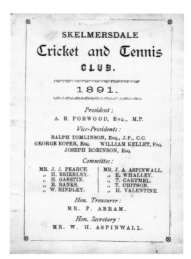

▼ The inaugural membership card from 1891.

SKELMERSDALE
Cricket and Tennis
CLUB.

1891.

President:
A. B. FORWOOD, Esq., M.P.
Vice-Presidents:
RALPH TOMLINSON, Esq., J.P., C.C.
GEORGE ROPER, Esq.   WILLIAM KELLET, Esq.
JOSEPH ROBINSON, Esq.
Committee:

MR. J. J. PEARCE.	MR. J. A. ASPINWALL.
,, H. BRIERLEY.	,, E. WHALLEY.
,, H. GARSTIN.	,, T. CARTMEL.
,, R. BANKS.	,, T. CHITSON.
,, W. HINDLEY.	,, H. VALENTINE.

Hon. Treasurer:
MR. P. ABRAM.
Hon. Secretary:
MR. W. H. ASPINWALL.

◄◄ ▲ Skelmersdale team from the early 1900s. Thomas Muldoon, fourth left, took 7 for 13 against Ormskirk.

◄◄ ▼ Management committee and players (1921–2) shortly before the purchase of the School Lane ground.

 Bill Wilson, Harry Thompson and Jim Bridge from the team that won Division Two of the Southport League in 1931.

BRITAIN'S LOST
CRICKET GROUNDS

116

 The Skelmersdale team circa 1930. A horse appears to be grazing the outfield.

outfield.' And the pitch itself? 'It was never easy to bat on, although it was a lot flatter than the rest of the ground. However good a fielder you were, the ball could always shoot up and make you look a fool.'

Club secretary Derek Lowe's entertaining online history of cricket in Skelmersdale records that the land – 4.746 hectares in all – was purchased in 1924 for £240 from Lord Lathom's estate, and that 'the contours were variable'. In 1935, the management minutes show, a Mr Briscoe and a Mr Hunter looked into the 'purchase of sheep' to keep the grass down. 'The cost of each sheep was quoted at between £13 and £15. This was thought to be too expensive and the two gentlemen were asked to continue with negotiations.'

The Mr Briscoe in question was a local butcher, as indeed was his son Bill, a team-mate of Alan's in the 1960s and '70s. 'He made the meat paste for the sandwiches that we had for every home game, come what may. But his wife served them quite daintily with the crusts cut off. I see the players today piling up their plates with pasta salad and heaven knows what, and think about those little sandwiches. You were lucky if you got two each.'

Tea to wash them down was served from an enormous urn in a somewhat functional pavilion that was renovated and extended over the years. Various strict Methodists resigned from the committee when a bar was added in the early 1970s. Alan and his brother John were among the players who helped to build it. They also helped to soften the appearance of the ground by acquiring some silver birch saplings from the side of the railway line after Dr Beeching closed the local station in 1963. The birch trees are still there, bordering a garden fence beyond the children's playground.

Farokh Engineer, the Lancashire and India wicketkeeper, officially opened the bar around the same time that the club made a breakthrough on the field. Skelmersdale won division one of the Southport and District League in 1973. Yet only the previous year, one Alan Pheasant had scored the first century at School Lane since the late 1950s.

Local folklore has it that a PC George Nutall hit a six into the grounds of the town hall from this site while compiling a brisk 142 for Ormskirk Police against Ormskirk Banks in the 1920s. It must have been a blow worthy of Wally Hammond, judging by the considerable distance to the site of the old town hall. The building itself has long gone, along with much else of any character in Skelmersdale. When the Forsters'

◀ Alan Forster batting at St Simon's in 1970.

▼ Skelmersdale second XI openers Bill Regan and Eddie Moss on their way to the crease at School Lane.

father, John senior, started playing here long before the war, it was a tight community of 7,000 souls or so. The cricket team was made up of farmers, miners and those who earned their living in factories making clogs, ropes or fireworks.

Today the population is five times bigger. 'Skem' became officially a 'new town' in the 1960s, attracting incomers from Liverpool and elsewhere. There are now a lot of houses, a lot of warehouses and not much else. And that makes the cricket club all the more precious as a rich repository of old Skem's soul. Skelmersdale CC has been 'strapped for brass', as they say round here, for most of its colourful history. But at least the money from The Willows – Headingley Close and all – has secured its future at a fine ground, with a level outfield and an expansive modern pavilion worthy of its new status in the Liverpool and District League.

Sometimes change really is for the better.

◀ Winners of Skelmersdale CC's knockout competition for local pubs and businesses. Stormy was a small area of 'Skem' boasting a school, 30 houses and three pubs.

22: RODNEY PARADE

A damp and drizzly day in Newport. The wet slate roofs are glossily grey and the River Usk looks murkily brown as it meanders sluggishly between broad mudflats. At least the taxi driver has a colourful turn of phrase. Asked to take us to Rodney Parade, he exclaims: 'Haven't they blown that fucking place up yet?' On the contrary. The abundance of lorries, cranes and drills around the home of the Newport Gwent Dragons indicates that the local rugby club is improving its facilities and the site of what was once the adjoining cricket ground is set for another round of redevelopment.

The last round began in the early 1990s, not too long after Glamorgan's final Sunday League game at Rodney Parade (against Yorkshire). Newport CC, who had played here for the previous century, decamped to a new 'sports village'. But not before playing a final friendly against Cardiff on 16 September 1990. At the end of the match, the bails were burnt and placed in an urn similar to the one at Lord's. The two clubs have competed for Wales's answer to the Ashes ever since.

Newport's ground is now at a place called Spytty Park, which sounds better when spoken in Welsh than it looks written down. 'The club has much better facilities now, and has a thriving youth and junior section,' says my genial guide, Andrew Hignell, Glamorgan's scorer and archivist. 'But it's out of town. I remember coming to Rodney Parade first in the 1970s and it always seemed a very vibrant place. It was so close to the city centre.'

Still is, of course. The centre is just over a rather stylish modern bridge from what is now known as the Crindau Gateway, promising a mixture of waterfront apartments, retail and commercial businesses, and given impetus by Newport's staging of the Ryder Cup in 2010. Some apartments have already been built. Beyond them is the site of a long-demolished power station where Wally Hammond once smashed a window.

◀◀ ▲ Glamorgan play at Rodney Parade on 6 June 1988. The umpire is former Glamorgan player Mervyn Kitchen.

◀◀ ▼ The Glamorgan team takes the field at Rodney Parade against Yorkshire in 1949.

▶ The Rodney Parade
ground shortly before the
final John Player League
game against Yorkshire was
rained off in 1990.

It was 1939 and Glamorgan were playing their first of two fixtures that year at Newport, having amalgamated with Monmouthshire four years previously. The home side posted a modest 196 in the first innings, whereupon Gloucestershire amassed 505 for 5 declared, with Hammond not out on 302. Wilf Wooller apparently described it as 'the worst triple century I've ever seen'. But his beloved Glamorgan refused to lie down – particularly their own star batsman of the day, Emrys Davies. He hit 287 not out (a county record for sixty-one years) as they replied with 557 for 4. The match was drawn. And the power station window? By all accounts, that was replaced only some time after the war and the broken pane was kept in the pavilion for many years. The southerly end of the ground was always known as the power station end (it's now an extended bus garage). The other was the pavilion end.

As the scores in that 1939 match suggest, Rodney Parade was considered a very good wicket. 'It was somewhere inside that school,' Andrew maintains. 'Straight ahead from here,' he adds, pointing through the gates. We don't bother wandering in. Two men entering a primary school uninvited these days could lead to the police being called. Or maybe I'm being made paranoid by the CCTV camera pointing at us from the back of the rugby ground's hospitality suites.

We're roughly where the handsome Edwardian pavilion once stood. 'It was very impressive, a real statement of civic pride,' Andrew confides. 'I'm quite surprised that they were allowed to demolish it.' Lord Tredegar must be turning in his grave. It was he who had it built in 1901, having already leased the Newport Athletic Club a further five acres to lay out a self-contained cricket ground. The club bought the freehold in 1922 and continued to make improvements. By the 1960s, however, falling attendances led to questions being asked about the viability of county cricket in Newport. The last

first-class match, against Warwickshire, took place in 1965. John Player League games returned in the late 1980s, however, as Andrew knows all too well. He was the Bill Frindall of Radio Wales in those days. What a shame that last game against Yorkshire in 1990 had to be abandoned without a ball being bowled.

'The Saturday was fine,' Newport secretary and scorer Phillip Stallard recalls. 'The ground looked an absolute picture with stands and advertising everywhere as it was due to be televised on the BBC.' Sunday, alas, was a different story. It had rained heavily overnight and it continued until mid-afternoon. 'Just as we were preparing to take the covers off,' Phil goes on, 'it started to rain again. This time it didn't stop.'

Another wet day in Newport had turned Glamorgan's last visit into a damp squib.

▼ Four spectators dressed for the Newport weather enjoy a fine view of the handsome Edwardian pavilion and some play as well.

Newport Cricket Club play at Rodney Parade on 6 June 1988.

23: ERINOID

▲ The superbly picturesque prospect of the Erinoid ground during the Stroud Cricket Festival in May 1960 for Gloucestershire's match with Surrey.

▶▶ The final benefit match played at the Erinoid ground in 1963 before its closure saw Richie Benaud (front left) turning out, along with then-England opening batsman Brian Bolus (fourth from left, with the centre parting). On Bolus's left is the Erinoid club captain Brian Ryland.

'Train stopped play' is a phrase rarely heard in first-class cricket. But apparently it happened one day at the former Erinoid ground in Stroud. I say 'apparently' because the source of this steamy tale was that irrepressible spinner of yarns as well as cricket balls, the late and much lamented Bryan 'Bomber' Wells. He was bowling for his native Gloucestershire back in the pre-diesel, pre-Beeching days when one end of the ground was known as the railway end. A train driver finding himself a little early on his approach to Stroud station stopped to watch the cricket for a while, seemingly unaware or unconcerned that smoke was issuing from the funnel at an alarming rate. Eventually the train moved on, but the smoke stayed behind, leaving players and spectators in a thick fog for some time.

'You never knew whether to believe dear old Bomber's stories or not,' chuckles Gloucestershire archivist Roger Gibbons as his Peugeot 207 turns into a cul-de-sac of semis, some of them in reconstituted Cotswold stone. 'I think this is where the pitch was,' ponders former Gloucestershire chairman John Light from the back seat. And a lively pitch it was, too, in the years between 1956 and 1963 when the ground adjoining the plastics factory of Erinoid staged first-class as well as club matches. It became known as 'Death Valley' to visiting batsmen, conscious of the hilly terrain around a wicket that was itself anything but flat. 'One day the seam bowlers would create mayhem; on another Bomber would come on and take four or five wickets,' Roger reflects. 'A sporting wicket, as M.J.K. Smith called it.'

M.J.K. was one of the few batsmen to make runs here – 182 not out in June 1959. 'I'll never forget it,' Warwickshire team-mate Tom Cartwright told his biographer Stephen Chalke. 'We all thought we were going home on the second night. The ball turned square; it shot along the ground; it went over your shoulder. It was the most amazing pitch.' John Light won't forget it either. He would have been a young man of nineteen at the time. Pointing out of the Peugeot's back window towards a clump of trees, he recalls: 'I remember Smith sweeping Sam Cook into the river over there,' he says, still shaking his head in disbelief. 'Nobody swept Sam like that. The crowd was stunned.'

Another of Gloucestershire's fabled spinners, David Allen, took eleven wickets here in 1963. 'The Erinoid match was always at the end of May or beginning of June and it was a good place to give your figures a boost before the Test selectors sat down,' he recalls. M.J.K. apart, most batsmen were less keen. 'I remember Dickie Bird walking past me at mid on after getting a pair, or not much more, when he was playing for Leicestershire,' David goes on. '"Eee, this is a hard way to earn a crust," he said as he headed back to the pavilion.'

The pavilion has long gone, as indeed has the Erinoid factory. Only the river flows on, harbouring in its depths perhaps the remains of a lost ball or two deposited there by the few batsmen to have prospered at Death Valley.

▲ Erinoid's Managing Director Derek Kleeman, seen here at the ground with Alec Bedser and Tom Graveney, was a pioneer of corporate hospitality in using Gloucestershire's festival visits as an opportunity to entertain customers.

24: STROUD

To lose one ground may be regarded as a misfortune, as Oscar Wilde might have put it. To lose two looks like carelessness. Or opportunity, as the officials of Stroud Cricket Club would put it. 'We've been looking for a new ground for twelve years,' says chairman Tony Elliott-Cannon as we look out, from an unusual pavilion that doubles as a children's nursery, over the sloping field of Farmhill, the club's home since the 1860s and soon to disappear under seventy-seven new houses. History would appear to be repeating itself twenty years or so after the old Erinoid factory ground, a mile or so across town, became another anonymous cul-de-sac.

There is a silver lining to this cloud over Stroud, however. 'We now run four sides, so it makes sense to have two pitches,' Tony goes on. 'And that's what we've got at our new place.' Ebley Meadows it's called, which sounds delightfully bucolic but probably isn't. 'It's down by the bypass,' Tony confirms. 'It's no more than two miles from here, plus we get some money in the bank.' Less of a slope, too? 'Definitely. And, believe me, it's difficult to find flat ground in this neck of the woods.' John Arlott once described Erinoid as 'a great amphitheatre, natural on three sides'. Here at Farmhill, there are similarly striking views of sharply rising ground beyond some local authority housing at what's known as the council house end.

That sloping pitch might explain why, unlike Erinoid, it has never hosted first-class cricket. But the club has developed many a Gloucestershire county player, including England's most artistic wicketkeeper. Jack Russell was an early beneficiary of the Stroud youth policy. 'I started with him back in 1977,' says Richard Cox, who's still playing at forty-six. 'Still bowling into the wind too,' he adds. 'I used to swing it about a bit, but Jack never missed many.'

A bit of an all-rounder is Richard: bowler, batsman and now club historian. He's compiling the story of a ground where Fred Grace, brother of W.G., played his last

◀◀ ▲ The Gloucestershire 1st X1 mingling with the Stroud team at Farmhill in 1931. Wally Hammond is second left.

◀◀ ▼ The Stroud team taking the field at Farmhill in 1953, led by Martin Cullimore who had played twice for Gloucestershire in 1929.

game for East Gloucestershire shortly before dying of pneumonia in 1880, and film director Jack Lee, brother of Laurie, batted for Stroud in the 1930s.

One of the distinguishing features of Farmhill was its old Victorian pavilion, built in distinctive Tyrolean style. Richard will never forget the day it suffered the fate of far too many pavilions – being razed to the ground, more often than not by vandals-turned-arsonists. 'It was my birthday in 2006, and I was woken up with the news that it was on fire,' he says, shaking his head. 'I remember Jack [Russell] coming down to have a look at the charred remains and he was very upset. He'd painted that pavilion.' With creosote? 'No, on canvas.'

These days, of course, Jack runs his own gallery at nearby Chipping Sodbury. It's there that I finally catch up with him. 'Even when I was a Test player,' he says, 'I'd go and sit on the bank by the side of the pavilion at the start of every season and imagine the ghosts of all those past Stroud players running about out there. It helped to keep my feet on the ground.' Talking of feet, he also remembers the splinters in the wooden floor of that pavilion. 'As soon as I could, I bagged my own corner to change in. When it burnt down, I asked them to search through the rubble for my peg, but there was nothing left.' And the painting, Jack: what happened to that? 'A bloke called Steve O'Brien bought it for his dad's birthday. Dougie O'Brien was the first-team wicket-keeper that I took over from in 1978.'

▼ A match at Farmhill in 1960.

◀ The distinctive Tyrolean pavilion painted in 2000 by Jill Austin, wife of the Warwickshire scorer.

Jack's beloved Tyrolean pavilion was replaced by something modern, shipped from Estonia in pack form, delivered on four big trucks and assembled IKEA-style. It looks like a log cabin and feels particularly well insulated on a cold and wet winter's day. Are the facilities better than those of the old pavilion?

'Just a bit,' snorts chairman Tony over the whoops, shrieks and laughter of children in the adjoining nursery, run by his wife Kate. 'We had to make it multi-functional,' he goes on, 'because there wasn't enough money from the insurance pay-out to do anything else.' And will the Estonian log cabin be taken down and reassembled at Ebley Meadows?

'No. It'll stay here as the nursery. I'm going to Finland to get us a new pavilion.'

◀ The President's XI v Chairman's XI match, 1987 with Jack Russell behind the stumps..

25: STANFORD HALL

Nick Shaw is not difficult to spot outside Loughborough station. The secretary of Wymeswold Cricket Club, six foot three in a sleeveless cricket sweater over a T-shirt, bears a marked resemblance to the comedian Harry Hill. He drives more like Damon Hill. But we arrive at Stanford Hall on the Nottinghamshire–Leicestershire border in one piece, sail through the gates and down the drive. 'There it is,' says Nick excitedly. Soon he's striding ahead, peering into the grass in search of something – anything – to indicate that this was once the most fabled country house cricket venue in the land. All we can see are a few straggly dandelions and some golden leaves bowling along in a mild autumnal breeze. A stout oak at deep square leg is one of an array of deciduous trees ranged around what used to be the boundary.

'We started playing here in the late seventies when our club was known as Rempstone,' Nick goes on. 'It was properly maintained then – a beautiful wicket and outfield.' But its heyday had been fifty summers earlier when Sir Julien Cahn owned the Georgian hall and the 3,000 acres around it. Sir Julien made his fortune in the hire purchase furniture business. He was a philanthropist as well as president and bankroller of Nottinghamshire CCC. What's more, he was prepared to pay for some of the world's finest cricketers to come and play Sunday matches on his doorstep. And not just to watch them: Cahn expected to play. Yet, as *The Cricketer* magazine observed in September 1997, he was 'at once the most prolific patron of cricket between the wars and comfortably the worst-ever first-class cricketer'.

J.M. Barrie, who briefly worked as a journalist in Nottingham before going on to write *Peter Pan*, once observed that Sir Julien's deliveries were so slow that if he didn't like one he could run after it and fetch it back. But at least there was an element of surprise in the occasional ball from Cahn – the one that climbed so high that the batsman seemed to have forgotten that it was up there. How else do we explain his dismissal of Kumar Shri

◀◀ ▲ Sir Julien Cahn flanked by F.C.W. Newman of Surrey (left) and R.C. Blunt of New Zealand. D.B.R. Morkel of Nottinghamshire and South Africa is on the far left of the front row.

◀◀ ▼ Cricket at Stanford Hall in the 1980s. The batsman is attempting a 'greenhouse' shot.

Duleepsinhji (Cambridge University, Sussex and England)? 'Halfway through the ball's flight, Duleepsinhji seemed to lose interest and sat on the end of his bat handle awaiting a return from outer space,' writes Cahn's biographer Miranda Rijks. 'The look of consternation on his face when the ball landed on top of two trembling bails was a picture indeed.'

Even more remarkable was Sir Julien's apparent hold over Frank Woolley of Kent and England, widely regarded as one of the most elegant left-handers of his or any other time. Cahn trapped him on more than one occasion and would always bring himself on to bowl when Woolley came in, muttering to fellow members of the Sir Julien Cahn XI: 'Here comes my rabbit.'

Such triumphs with the ball were rare indeed for the 'Eccentric Entrepreneur', as Rijks dubbed him in the title of her biography. The six balls with which he took wickets in a career that spanned at least thirteen seasons (not to mention winter tours of the 'dominions' with his almost invincible XI) were mounted on silver plinths and displayed in the library at Stanford Hall.

Sir Julien was no better at other aspects of the game. He took evasive action if the ball came anywhere near him in the field, and when going into bat he took the precaution of donning inflatable pads, blown to a pressure of 23lb all round by Robson, chauffeur of his Rolls-Royce Phantom 2. 'Deliveries flew off the pads like a tennis ball thrown against a brick wall,' writes Duncan Hamilton in his biography of Harold Larwood, one of several Notts players whom the president supported financially and unofficially. 'But no umpire dared give a leg bye against Cahn when he was batting.'

Between 1926 and 1939, Sir Julien lavished between £20,000 and £30,000 a year on local cricket, transforming Trent Bridge in the process. He had another ground, West Park, laid out within ten minutes' walk of the county headquarters and it was there that his XI took on touring teams from every country, apart from Australia, who would have been too big a draw for an occasion that was free to the public. It was in the elegant Lutyens-style pavilion at West Park that Sir Julien tried to persuade Larwood to sign an apology for the furore caused by the infamous 'bodyline' tour of 1932–3. To his eternal credit, the great bowler declined. But why was Cahn doing the MCC's dirty work? Perhaps he was desperate to ingratiate himself with an organisation that looked down on him as a Jew who made his money through trade. Anti-Semitism was as rife as snobbery among the English upper classes in the 1930s.

The pavilion is still there, thanks to a campaign led by Notts archivist and librarian Peter Wynne-Thomas which scuppered a scheme to build apartments on the site. The West Park pitch is still there too. It's now the headquarters of the West Bridgford British Legion team. They also played occasional games at Stanford Hall until around fifteen years ago, when the days of this illustrious country house ground were already numbered. 'It was a beautiful setting to play in, but there was no changing room and no showers,' recalls club secretary Chris Roper, who still stands behind the stumps at fifty-three, either as umpire or wicketkeeper. 'After a game on a hot day, some of our lads dived in the swimming pool to cool off.' That would be the same pool in which Lady Cahn, strapped for something to buy as a birthday present for the man who had everything, once installed a pair of sealions.

Chris learnt much about Sir Julien from his father, who played for the Legion before him. 'And my Uncle Eric,' he adds. 'He told me about the boat full of women moored on the Trent when touring teams came to Nottingham.' Idle talk? Well, possibly not. Rijks's biography mentions the women, if not the boat: 'Legend says that Sir Julien always provided ten girls for the opposing teams after major games. When asked why he only provided ten, the answer came: "Because the chap who got me out didn't get a girl."' He also

ensured that cricketing visitors to Stanford Hall were well wined and dined – particularly the opposition. On those rare occasions when his XI had a bad morning, opposing players would be detained over port and cigars for a period that far exceeded the norm for a cricketing lunch break. His own side were expected to observe strict quotas until after stumps were drawn. That may help to explain why they lost only nineteen of the 621 games they played until the outbreak of war in 1939. The major factor, however, was the quality of players he could call upon. His team that toured Jamaica in 1929, for instance, included Wilfred 'Dodge' Whysall of Notts, Ewart Astill of Leicestershire, Andy Sandham of Surrey and Lord Tennyson of Hampshire, grandson of the poet. England players all.

Sir Julian died in 1944. The following year, house and grounds were sold for £54,000. To the Co-op, as it happens, which used the Georgian mansion as a training school and, in keeping with more egalitarian times, offered the cricket pitch to local clubs. The Co-op finally sold up at the end of the century and, in 2009, the property developer Chek Whyte was granted planning permission to build a £60 million luxury retirement village on the site – only to see his plans undermined by mounting debts which he blamed on the recession. The hall is still there, shrouded in memories of more colourful days.

The same could be said of what was once the cricket pitch where Nick Shaw, having unsuccessfully scoured the undergrowth for signs of where the wicket used to be, is reliving a few memories of his playing days with Rempstone before it evolved into Wymeswold. 'I remember getting my highest score of eighty-something here, including a late cut from which we ran five. It's a long boundary down there,' he adds, pointing to a distant wall over which outhouses protrude, including some greenhouse roofs. The nursery end, you might say. 'As secretary, the Co-op asked me to take out insurance in case somebody put a six through one of them,' he goes on. 'But I never did. We managed to hit it twice and they only billed us once – for forty quid. Whenever someone bowled rubbish, though, we always called it a 'greenhouse ball'.'

As we set off back down the drive, I can't help wondering what the glass bill must have been like when Sir Julien was tossing up greenhouse balls to some of the world's greatest batsmen.

 A view from the 'nursery' end during a match at Stanford Hall during the 1980s.

26: BEESTON

▲ An office block now occupies the site of Beeston's Meadow Road Ground.

Beeston is the first stop out of Nottingham on the main line to St Pancras. It boasts a handsome little Victorian station with an equally handsome Victorian pub off platform 1. Appropriately enough, it's called the Victoria Hotel and, believe me, there aren't too many better places to enjoy a post-match pint.

Supporters of Nottingham rugby knew that all too well until the club decamped from Beeston to Notts County's Meadow Lane a few years ago. Coincidentally, Meadow Road cricket ground (no relation) lay across the railway line from the 'Vic', as the pub is known locally. The last match played there, however, was around fifty years ago when Nottinghamshire Youth took on Derbyshire Juniors. In 1961, the landlords, Ericssons Telephones Ltd, were taken over by Plessey, who were in the vanguard of what Harold Wilson would later call the 'white heat of technology'. New buildings were required and the cricket ground disappeared, while the works team moved to a pitch down the road. By that time, Meadow Road was not far off its century. The first

▶ The Ericssons team of 1950 at Meadow Road.

recorded match was in 1867, when the Gentlemen of Nottinghamshire played the Gentlemen of Lincolnshire.

By far the most celebrated game ever played here came three years later when Beeston hosted its only first-class contest. The Gentlemen of the South played the Gentlemen of the North in what turned out to be, as one excitable scribe put it, 'the greatest run-getting match of 1870', adding: 'In all, 1,114 runs were scored for 31 wickets, a most remarkable performance.'

Two of the three cricketing Grace brothers turned out for the South and, on this occasion, G.F. outshone W.G. with the bat. He scored 189 in a first innings total of 482, compared to the artful doctor's mere 77. W.G. starred with the ball, however, taking five wickets in the North's first innings of 287 all out and four in their second of 289. 'The South had only 59 runs to get,' the scribe goes on, 'when time was called to enable them to catch the train.'

For most of its nigh-on 100 years existence, Manor Road was a works ground for the adjoining factory. 'There were seven thousand employees at Ericssons at one time,' says Steve Hodgkinson, maintenance man at the Vic. 'My dad was one of them. He worked there before and after the war and bowled fast for the cricket team.'

Bob Hodgkinson is by far the tallest man on the back row of a team shot taken in 1954, when the works team won what Steve believes was the Popkess Cup. (It was named after the Chief Constable of Nottingham, who went under the splendid title of Captain Athelstan Popkess.) Steve himself is too young to remember much about the ground. 'But my older sister Pamela used to score for them. She's no longer with us,' he adds with understandable sadness.

From the footbridge over the railway line, the view is anything but handsome. A rectangular office block now dominates a business park that is part of HSBC's investment arm. Somewhere behind or beneath that soulless building is the ground that once hosted the biggest run-fest of 1870 – a rum thought to conjure with as I rush off to catch the southbound train approaching platform 2.

▼ The scorecard for the only first-class match ever played at Meadow Road, Beeston, in 1870.

Other Matches.	406	Other Matches.

GENTLEMEN OF THE NORTH v. GENTLEMEN OF THE SOUTH.

Beeston, August 18, 19, & 20, 1870.

This was the first visit of Mr. W. G. Grace to the vicinity of Nottingham, and his presence, coupled with fine weather, attracted a very large and fashionable crowd. The contest has left its mark on cricket history as the greatest run-getting match of 1870. In all, 1,114 runs were scored for 31 wickets, a most remarkable performance. Mr. Hornby's 103 included one 8 and seventeen 4's; Mr. I. D. Walker's 77 was a brilliant innings, but both these were surpassed by Mr. I. D. Walker's 179, in which he hit one 5 and twenty-five 4's, and Mr. G. F. Grace's 189, which included thirty-five 4's. The other eight batsmen, for the South, made 19 between them. Mr. W. G. Grace records that Mr. Strachan waited patiently to go in with his pads on for six hours, only then to be dismissed second ball. The South had only 59 runs to get when time was called to enable them to catch the train. Score :—

GENTS. OF NORTH.	First Innings		Second Innings
J. W. Dale, c Day, b W. G. Grace	19	b Rutter	19
A. N. Hornby, b Strachan	103	c sub., b W. G. Grace	8
J. G. Beevor, b W. G. Grace	1	l b w, b Strachan	59
C. Smith, b W. G. Grace	43	b W. G. Grace	13
C. W. Walker, c and b W. G. Grace	19	b G. F. Grace	40
D. W. Mackinnon, b W. G. Grace	5	c G. F. Grace, b Walker	42
F. C. Cobden, st Martin, b Strachan	19	not out	32
J. W. B. Whettam, c Martin, b W. G. Grace	7	b G. F. Grace	5
E. M. Riddell, b C. J. Thornton	36	c Martin, b Rutter	30
A. Appleby, c sub, b G. F. Grace	16	l b w, b W. G. Grace	18
C. Ashwell, not out	2	b Rutter	19
Byes 9, leg byes 7, wide 1	17	Bye 1, leg byes 2, wide 1	4
	287		289

GENTS. OF THE SOUTH.	First Innings		First Innings
W. G. Grace, c Hornby, b Mackinnon	77	not out	29
P. M. Thornton, b Appleby	2		
C. J. Thornton, l b w, b Appleby	0		
I. D. Walker, c Smith, b Hornby	179	b Mackinnon	18
G. F. Grace, not out	189		
G. Strachan, c and b Hornby	2		
M. T. Martin, l b w, b Appleby	6		
G. Fillingham, c Riddell, b Hornby	0		
E. Rutter, b Appleby	0		
J. J. Day, c Mackinnon, b Hornby	9		
M. J. Hall, b Appleby	0		
Byes 9, leg byes 7, wides 2	18	Byes 8, leg bye 1	9
	482		56

Umpires—F. Tinley & J. Buttery.

▼ The 1954 Ericsson's Team. Bob Hodgkinson is the tallest player in the back row.

27: CRABBLE

Every cricketer has a favourite ground, as Ray Illingworth points out in his autobiography *From Yorkshire and Back*. That hard-headed Tyke's field of dreams turns out to have been a lot further south than Bradford or Bramall Lane, surprisingly enough, and closer to Calais than to London. Why Dover? 'I always felt the setting was delightful and the sun always seemed to shine,' Illy trills. Oh, yes, and he just happened to score 135 in Yorkshire's only innings and take 7 for 49 followed by 7 for 52 as Kent slumped to defeat by an innings and 13 runs in August 1964.

'It was a bit of a spinner's paradise at one time,' says Ray Durrant, sixty, an all-rounder himself, who played for Dover between 1968 and 1995. His old pal and teammate Mick Palmer nods concurrence before adding: 'I think Geoff Miller sealed his place in the Test team on the back of his performance here.' Since you ask, Miller took 7 for 74 in Kent's second innings and 4 for 66 in the first. And still Derbyshire lost by 62 runs – which meant that Kent finished its nigh-on seventy-year association with Dover with a victory on a July day in the scorching summer of '76. A county with more out grounds than most was following the national trend for playing the bulk of its matches at headquarters. Whether that was to maximise revenue or to cut the number of two-day finishes on a pitch that too often started to break up on the second day matters not, thirty-five years on. The plain fact is that they ain't coming back. Not Kent CCC, nor Dover CC. The club wound itself up.

'We played our last match on the twenty-third of August 2003,' says Mick, who gives the impression that the date is engraved on his heart. He's still playing at a lower level at sixty-three, but Dover's Crabble ground is all too evidently a special place for him. I can see why as we gaze out from steps half way up the steep, almost cliff-like bank dug out of a chalk down towards the end of the nineteenth century to form an amphitheatre for cricket, football, rugby and cycling. Over 110 years on and Dover

◀◀ ▲ Colin Cowdrey pulls on his gloves as he strides to the Crabble crease in on 30 August 1967 as Kent play Warwickshire at the Crabble Athletic Ground.

◀◀ ▼ Crabble today with the handsome flint-built pavilion-cum-clubhouse looking out over only rugby fields.

KENT C.C. DOVER. 1912.

▲ The Kent team at Dover in 1912.

Athletic FC have a separate ground at the top of the hill while rugby pitches are spread across the expansive field in front of us, winter and summer. The days when Dover RFC handed over the keys of the handsome flint-built clubhouse-cum-pavilion every spring and received them back every September have gone.

'I knew there was no chance of us ever coming back when I saw those floodlights,' says Ray sadly, pointing to a row of pylons between pitches. 'That's where the main square was. But there were five pitches altogether and sometimes there'd be a first and second team game going on simultaneously. You could be fielding on the boundary and a ball from another match might come whistling past your ear.'

The club pitches were laid out east to west with the river end on one side and the Dover end at the other. 'You tried very hard not to be batting as the sun went down,' Ray confides. 'Only in exceptional circumstances did you put the opposition in if you won the toss.' The county pitch was aligned from north to south with a fairly marked slope at the southerly end, as Ray discovered when the county withdrew and the club's first team played on that track. 'It was a fair old slog bowling up hill,' Ray concedes, peering across at it from his impressive height. 'You think I'm tall now,' he adds wryly, 'but I was six foot ten before I started running up that hill from the scoreboard end.'

That main scoreboard has long gone. Only a smaller, green hut remains on the other side of the ground, about a third of the way up the 'cliff face' and reached by steep stone steps. The letters are faded now, but you can just about make out the words WICKETS, OVERS and TOTAL. 'They used to keep in touch with the main box by

◀ James Seymour at Dover in 1921.

▼ The Dover pavilion and stands in 1889.

CRABBLE

139

wind-up phone,' says Mick. That would have been advanced technology back in 1937, when Godfrey Evans was working the scoreboard as a ground-staff boy. It just happened to be the game where Kent scored 219 in seventy-one minutes to overhaul Gloucestershire. 'That, he used to claim, was more of a test of his agility – and mathematics – for him than coping with Alec Bedser's late swingers,' wrote David Foot in Evans's obituary in the *Guardian*.

Lifelong Kent fan John Williams was at that Gloucestershire game and will never forget it. He was ten at the time. Now eighty-five, he looks back on those pre-war Crabble days with great fondness – 'the various sized tents, the local stall holders, vendors of all sorts, soft cushion seats for hire at threepence a day, the pro cricketers emerging from the lower pavilion and the amateurs in their highly coloured cravats and caps from the dressing room upstairs'.

There wasn't much chance of the wicket breaking up early in those days. 'The county square was always cordoned off and religiously protected by six or so groundsmen,' John recalls. 'We got to know it as the "holy ground" and you ventured upon it at your peril.' He played for Dover himself in the mid-1950s and maintains that the wicket had already begun to deteriorate by then. (Great players could still make runs on it, as Gary Sobers proved by hitting the fastest century of the season in 1968.)

Quite how the club itself deteriorated is a complicated story. Dover won the Kent League twice in the 1980s and was still able to attract an overseas player of the calibre of Australia's Justin Langer as late as 1992. Ray and Mick struggle to come up with a single reason for the descent into financial hardship in just over ten years. A major contributor, however, was the debt the cricket club ended up owing to the brewery for their half of a joint venture to build a new bar in the members' section of the old

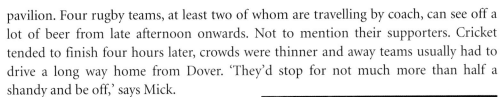

pavilion. Four rugby teams, at least two of whom are travelling by coach, can see off a lot of beer from late afternoon onwards. Not to mention their supporters. Cricket tended to finish four hours later, crowds were thinner and away teams usually had to drive a long way home from Dover. 'They'd stop for not much more than half a shandy and be off,' says Mick.

Things were very different in the 1960s, when the beer tent was well used during and long after county matches. 'The away teams were staying over in Dover and didn't have much else to do,' Ray suggests. Sometimes the quest for cheaper beer would lead a visiting team to leave the port on what was known locally as a 'non-lander' – a ferry that would move three miles off shore to allow duty-free prices and non-existent closing times.

Perhaps those early Crabble finishes in the post-war years occasionally had as much to do with scrambled brains as crumbling pitches.

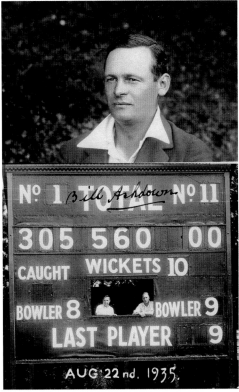

  An aerial view of a county match in the 1920s.

◀ Bill Ashdown after scoring the highest total ever scored at the Crabble: 305 not out against Derby in 1935.

Tea for two and a bird's eye view of Crabble cricket during a pre-war county week.

28: ROYAL HIGH

Although Scotland has traditionally punched above its weight on the football field and produced a disproportionate number of top football managers, it has never been regarded as a cradle of cricket. Yet the game has been played there for over 225 years and there are currently thirty-two clubs in the national league, while between two and three hundred play in regional leagues. Scots will point out that Mike Denness (born in North Lanarkshire) captained England nineteen times and they claim Douglas Jardine as one of their own. Well, he was born in what was then Bombay to Scottish parents – pedigree enough for one prominent Scottish cricket blogger to refer to him matily as 'Doug Jardine'.

Even the Scottish Parliament building in Edinburgh is partially built on a former cricket ground. Holyrood Field was granted to the Royal High School by Queen Victoria in 1861 and the current Royal High Cricket Club evolved from the old boys who played there for the next sixty years. According to Cricket Scotland historian Neil Leitch, they used to draw good-sized crowds, largely made up of 'Hibs-type supporters' from the nearby area known as Little Ireland. 'They didn't have to pay to get in,' says Neil, an old boy himself and still official club scorer.

In 1921, Royal High moved to the suburb of Jock's Lodge, named after a shepherd who was resident there in the early 1600s. But school cricket continued at Holyrood until the late 1960s, when one of Edinburgh's most venerable educational institutions (founded 1128) moved out of the middle of town.

Neil was a pupil there at the time and he was scorer even in those days. 'I've always loved cricket but never been much good at playing it,' he explains. 'Perhaps that's because I was a prop forward. We were never renowned for being well co-ordinated.' He vividly remembers getting changed for rugby in the old pavilion, which hadn't been modernised since the senior cricketers left nearly fifty years before. 'There was one cold tap to wash the mud off,' he confides.

◀◀ ▲ The magnificent prospect of the Royal High cricket ground at Holyrood in Edinburgh, overlooked by Salisbury Crags.

◀◀ ▼ The same view nowadays, now occupied by the grounds of the Scottish Parliament.

▲ The Royal High School cricket team at the Holyrood ground in 1902, sitting on or near the square.

▶ The Royal High School team of 1904 in front of the pavilion.

At least he has fond memories of the summer months, marking dot balls and boundaries surrounded by Edinburgh's historic buildings, with the smell of hops wafting over the wall of the brewery that once stood opposite what is now the Parliament building. 'When the school moved out,' he says, 'the field reverted to the Crown and the pavilion became a place for the gardener to store tools. Part of the old ground is still there as just a little patch of grass. I remember [former Foreign Secretary] Robin Cook eyeing it when he was featured on the television news looking at plans for the new Parliament. "Oh," he exclaimed, "I used to play rugby on that field."'

Cook was an old boy of the Royal High, needless to say. So, too, was the comedian Ronnie Corbett. Indeed, Corbett was scorer for the school cricket team just after the Second World War. 'The only story I heard about him was from one of our players from the seventies who used to watch the school team play when he was very young,' Neil goes on. 'He went over to ask if Don Bradman was playing and was told to "run away, little boy".'

A facetious question, undoubtedly. But then he must have been very young and very small to be addressed as 'little boy' by Ronnie Corbett.

▲ RHS boys v RHS masters match in 1910.
▼ Holyrood Park in 1994 showing the ovoid outline of the Royal High ground.

BOWLEY

yours faithfully
L. L. Bowley
1909

29: DUDLEY

Spectators entered Dudley cricket ground at their own risk. It wasn't so much the threat of aerial bombardment from Wally Hammond or Ted Dexter in full flow – that could be a fact of life on any ground. No, the danger here came from below. Long before health and safety became something of an obsession for officials and jobsworths, notices appeared pointing out the possibility that the earth might move for you, the paying public. Subsidence was the problem. Around 1957 the authorities became aware that the ground that had hosted so many great club and Worcestershire county matches in the previous 117 years was resting on nothing more than a crust of earth suspended over hollow caves and small lakes.

The Earl of Dudley, it seems, had donated the land to lay out the pitch back in 1840. Did he mention that there were limestone workings underneath it? Who knows? All we do know is that large cracks appeared in the outfield as long ago as 1911, when Worcestershire were scheduled to play their first county games there, against Yorkshire in May and Lancashire the following month. Both had to be hastily rescheduled – one back to the main county ground at New Road, Worcester, and the other to Stourbridge. 'Eventually, in August, the [Dudley] ground was fit enough to stage a game against Gloucestershire,' writes Les Hatton in his booklet *Cricket Grounds of Worcestershire*. He goes on to record that there was a civic lunch at the nearby Station Hotel on the opening day, attended by various local worthies and the Gloucestershire captain, that mighty smiter Gilbert Jessop. Also present was Jessop's team-mate Wilf Brownlee, who returned fortified enough to hit the first six in first-class cricket at Dudley.

◄◄ Fred Bowley taking guard in 1909. Six years later he would make the highest score by a Worcestershire player at Dudley: 276 against Hampshire.

The first of many, as it turned out – although three years later, just before the outbreak of the First World War, Warwickshire's Frank Foster managed to hit 305 in 260 minutes without a single six. (There were forty-four fours and one five.) Twenty years later another Gloucestershire man, Wally Hammond, hit six sixes while compiling 265 not out. And a year before the next world war, the always voluble Dudley crowd was giving 'the bird' to Percy Chapman of Kent for batting too slowly. Chapman duly doffed his cap before smashing the next ball over the pavilion. There were plenty more big hits in postwar Dudley, but the former Sussex all-rounder Alan Oakman remembers one in particular. '[Ted] Dexter hit [Jack] Flavell back over his head and out of the ground,' he recalls.

More used to the fresh sea air of Hove, Oakman admits that the Sussex players rarely relished a trip to Dudley. OK, the ground was overlooked by the ruins of a medieval castle, but it wasn't exactly Arundel. Even some locals could understand the lack of enthusiasm from visiting teams. 'The panorama to the east was a devastating shock of the utmost industrial kind,' Patrick Talbot reminisced in an article for *The Blackcountryman*. 'It was draughty to boot. At 700 feet above sea level, it was at least a sleeveless sweater cooler than the county headquarters in that charming vale of Severn. Dudley's outfield always seemed littered with dumpy figures in at least two layers of sweaters. Other than an imposing black and white pavilion and a rickety stand at right angles to the square, the ground was very flat and open.'

Well, that's how it seemed to young Talbot, as he was in the 1960s when D'Oliveira and Gifford, Coldwell and Kenyon were in their prime. Now fifty-seven and a school teacher living in Staines, he also remembers one 'Curly', the scorecard seller who migrated to Dudley from Worcester whenever the county side came to play. 'He circulated the pitch, joking with the crowd in a broad, rustic voice. The back of his battered trilby couldn't hide the wayward strands of curly grey hair, and he had the ability to keep a thin, self-rolled cigarette in the corner of his mouth through all his conversations. Meanwhile, the local newspaper vendor proclaimed his presence with the poetic: "here we are, here we are, the man with the *Express and Star*".'

Dudley has always seen itself as the unofficial capital of the Black Country – 'a teardrop of land surrounded by Staffordshire', as Keith Cartwright, father of the novelist Anthony Cartwright, once told me. 'It was a symbol of our uniqueness geographically and people were very proud of the fact. When Worcestershire came to play here, it was an event.'

All that came to an end in 1977 when the county played their last John Player League match in Dudley against Nottinghamshire. The continuing fears over safety that had brought about that decision were finally proved to be well founded eight years later. On Saturday 25 May 1985, Dudley Cricket Club were about to play Aston Unity in a Birmingham league fixture. Morale was high, as Dudley topped that extremely competitive table. The ground staff were preparing the wicket when club manager Jack Sedgley found a large depression in the outfield. The fixture was quickly switched but, later in the day, the depression grew into a hole, forty feet across. Enough to close for good not only the cricket ground but also the adjoining football pitch, home to Dudley Town FC. At a stroke went two sources of local pride at a time when local factories and foundries were shutting down right, left and centre.

Nearly twenty-five years later, I walked past that site with Anthony Cartwright as he talked about his novel, *Heartland*, set in a fictional representation of his native Dudley.

Limestone workings or not, the two sports grounds had been obliterated by the sort of development that could be found on the edge of town anywhere in the United Kingdom or the United States. We shook our heads and walked on.

The following year I went back to have a closer look. Surely there must be something – a plaque, perhaps – to mark the fact that great cricketing deeds had been performed on this site. Not a thing. Not in the car park of the drive-through McDonalds where Worcestershire archivist Tim Jones believes the pitch might have been, 'as near as damn it'. Not on Nando's, Pizza Hut, the multiplex cinema, the adjoining business park or a pub called, with a developer's patronising nod to local sensibilities, the Bostin' Fittle. (That's Black Country for good food, in case you're wondering, and they offer seven different curries on a Thursday evening in case you're interested.) Nothing then to say that this was where George Parr led an All England XI against the twenty-two of Dudley in 1854; where 'Patsy' Hendren scored 301 not out for Middlesex in 1933; where 'Roly' Jenkins took fifteen Sussex wickets for 122 in 1953. Not even an acknowledgement that the great George Headley – second only to Bradman in the all-time batting averages until Graeme Pollock sneaked ahead of him by a decimal point – was a club professional here in the 1950s.

George died two years before the ground was closed. But his son Ron, now seventy-one, played for Worcestershire with distinction and still lives nearby. 'We have a Black Country museum to replicate the industry that no longer exists around here, but nothing to commemorate the cricket,' he says. 'For me, playing at Dudley was like coming home.' Never more so than in 1971 when Worcestershire beat local rivals Warwickshire to lift the John Player League under his captaincy. 'I got a few that day,' he recalls. In fact, he made a quick-fire fifty to turn the game Worcestershire's way. John Arlott and Jim Laker were there with a television crew. So were thousands of supporters from both sides of the county border. 'There wasn't a seat to be had,' says Ron.

Every one of them entered at their own risk and lived to tell the tale of a memorable match.

▲ The pavilion over which Percy Chapman of Kent smashed a six after being given the bird by the Dudley crowd.

30: GUINNESS

Guinness was good to you if you happened to be a useful cricketer when the old Park Royal sports ground was in its pomp. 'The small, pre-war wooden pavilion was always well stocked with crates of stout and the hospitality was very good,' recalls seventy-year-old John Lindley, playing even today for the still-thriving Ealing Cricket Club on the other side of the Hanger Lane Gyratory System.

He would have been six in 1947 when the accompanying picture was taken. 'I used to walk around the perimeter with my father on Sundays,' he explains. Little could he have known then that he would eventually play on this pitch, good enough to host Middlesex second XI cricket as well as games involving touring teams. 'These days I bowl off four paces, but I'm six foot four and I can still put it in places where the batsman doesn't like it,' he tells me before rushing off for his 'high-impact' aerobics class. Every summer Saturday he travels back to west London from his current home in Dorset to improve on a wicket tally that stood at 4,051 at the beginning of the 2011 season. And every time he passes Park Royal, he feels a twinge of regret as work progresses on preparing the former brewery sports ground for yet another industrial estate. The giant drinks company Diageo now owns the site where Guinness ceased brewing in 2005.

John remembers playing at Park Royal many times, including once for the forerunner of the Middlesex Cricket Board against Holland in the mid-1970s. 'I always liked to bowl from the pavilion end with the brewery on my left, and it was no different on that occasion. We lost on the fifth ball of the last over. For twenty years I worked just across the road, in the financial department at Visnews, at a time when there were plenty of works grounds within a ten-mile radius.'

Heinz, Barclays Bank, Pears Soap, Cherry Blossom boot polish and Sandersons wallpaper were among them. 'Guinness had a fine side because they always employed a fair number of good sportsmen,' he says. 'Brian Statham was on the sales force for a while after he packed up playing for Lancashire. Then there was Jim McConnon [the Glamorgan and England off-spinner], who worked and played alongside Statham. Oh yes, and "Pom Pom" Fellows-Smith, who also played rugby for South Africa.'

Last but not least there was Eddie Ingram, who like Guinness itself represented Ireland. Indeed he took five wickets for his country against Bradman's Australians in 1938. Two years previously he'd moved from the Dublin brewery to Park Royal. After the war, he briefly played for Middlesex, gaining his county cap in 1947. Later he played for Ealing and for Guinness as required. 'He was a very convivial character,' John recalls. 'Quite slim when I first knew him, he ballooned a bit later in his career.' In the 1986 *Wisden Book of Obituaries*, Benny Green described Ingram as 'a great character of Pickwickian girth'.

Too much Guinness hospitality, perhaps, in the days before high impact aerobics.

▼ The end-of-season match between the Guinness cricket and tennis clubs at Park Royal in 1948. The cricket club won, but only narrowly.

31: LITTLETOWN

▲ A post- First World War shot of the cricket team outside Hornsby House in Littletown.

Littletown is not a town at all. It's not even a village. Rather it's a hamlet of fifty-four houses, five miles east of Durham on a road to nowhere in particular. The local colliery closed in 1914 and the pub in more recent years. There is a village green but not much else. No shop, no school, no phone box. No cricket ground either since 2007, when pretty well the last focus of community activity was put out to grass after 120 years.

The Church Commissioners, who own the land, wanted to increase the lease and up the rent. 'The club didn't have the membership or the funds,' says Marion Allport, parish councillor and secretary of the residents' association. 'By that time they relied on outsiders to keep the team going. Back in the fifties it was very much a local side.' Among them was one Johnny Goodchild, who went on to play football for Sunderland, scoring twenty-one goals in forty-four games. He was a useful cricketer, too, making the Littletown team at fourteen and Durham county seconds by the time he was twenty

Not long after Goodchild scored a hat-trick against Leeds in his last game for Sunderland in 1961, Ron Young was preparing to play his first cricket match for the pit village of South Hetton. Now sixty-five and working for the Durham Cricket Board, he remembers making epic journeys to play Littletown when it was a 'thriving and successful' club. The distance was negligible, but the trip involved catching three buses with his youthful team-mates, all lugging bulging cricket bags. 'We couldn't afford to hire a coach,' Ron remembers. 'And one of the few blokes with a car in our village owned a pop factory and liked to have a couple of beers on the way to the game. My old man was his drinking mate and the only one he gave a lift to.

'When we got off the last bus, we had to go round the back of some old mining terraces where there were open fields. The cricket ground was one of them. The outfield was a bit up and down but the wicket was OK. I remember scoring some runs on it anyway. We went to the pub afterwards. If you were with the second team, as I was in those days, we could only run to halves – or "gills" as we call them up here – before catching the first of our buses home.'

The pub, known at different times as the Duke of York, the Ramblers' Rest and the Mystic Manor, supplied the teams with teas. Although some effort had been made to upgrade the 100-year-old, brick-built pavilion, it couldn't run to catering facilities.

In Ron's day, the Littletown team still included a fair number of miners who travelled to pits in neighbouring villages. 'I remember a bloke called David Higgins who bowled lively away swingers and could hit the ball really hard. He never wore batting gloves.'

Another useful player was Mark Nelson, who scored 10,000 runs in 400 games for Littletown. 'From around 1986, a lot of players of the same age came in and we fielded two sides every week,' he told the *Northern Echo* after the Church Commissioners had tolled the death knell. 'The flip side was that we all grew old together. We knew we had a limited shelf life. Players were getting injured or going off with their families and there were no youngsters. The village was too small and there was no one to recruit.'

Mark went on to play for Washington, but looked back fondly on the days when he walked out to bat much closer to home. 'They were a great set of lads and a lovely club. It's been a cricket field all this time and it'll be terrible to see long grass in Littletown.'

But long grass there is, four years on. Attempts by the Durham Cricket Board to find another team that could afford the new lease came to nothing. 'The last time I looked,' says cricket development manager Graeme Weeks, 'it was over two foot tall.'

Put out to grass indeed.

▼ An early-twentieth-century Littletown team pictured near the pavilion.

Littletown's cricket ground in 2007, put out to grass by the Church Commissioners. The forlornly abandoned roller has a job to do if cricket were ever to return. Note the cricketers painted on the pavilion doors.

'No Cricket' is the stern exhortation on the sign nowadays greeting would-be batsmen and bowlers at the empty expanse of Fartown.

32: FARTOWN

The clock stopped at 4.27. Who knows in which year? The faded grandeur of the half-timbered pavilion that the clock fronts is partially obscured by one of those leylandii trees that seem to grow a foot taller every two hours. Since cricket went into decline here at Fartown, Huddersfield, the building has been a night club and, more recently, the headquarters of the local Muslim Association.

The setting seems particularly bleak on a blustery Thursday morning with rain clouds rolling in over distant hills. Looking at the muddy rugby league pitch in front of us, it's difficult to take in that this was once considered among the finest wickets in all Yorkshire.

The county played first-class matches here from 1873 until 1955, when it was deemed to be Middlesbrough's turn for a regular visit. But John Player League games came back to Fartown from 1969 until 1982.

'The Great Triumvirate' of George Hirst, Wilfred Rhodes and Schofield Haigh are commemorated on the edge of the ground by a tall monument in local stone, topped by Old Father Time. All three were born locally. Originally dedicated to Hirst alone and sadly neglected, its restoration was one of the few bright glimmers on the Fartown horizon as decline gathered pace in the 1980s and '90s.

Yorkshire's decision to pull out in 1982 was preceded by one or two embarrassing episodes, including toilet blockages. Enter a new owner for the ground. As local cricket historian Steven Draper points out, 'his only interest seems to have been in turning the pavilion into a night club and turfing out the cricketers in the process.' What had been Huddersfield Cricket and Athletic Club broke up. The majority joined with Lockwood CC to play at the ICI ground on Leeds Road.

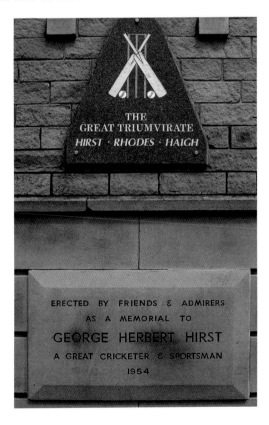

▼ The impressive monument at Fartown to the colossi of Yorkshire cricket.

▲ The terraced streets of
Huddersfield climb away
behind the Fartown pavilion.

A few stayed at Fartown for a 'disastrous' 1986 season, as Draper puts it, before folding altogether.

The cricketers of Edgerton, a rather more salubrious part of Huddersfield than Fartown, took over the ground for just above a decade. But the decline in its surroundings continued – not helped when the Huddersfield Giants rugby league side decamped to a stylish new stadium in 1992. (Only junior Giants and reserves still play here.) Responsibility for keeping the cricket square in good order fell to Kirklees Council and it's fair to say that it failed lamentably in that regard, citing budget cuts as an excuse. Edgerton duly left in 1997.

Cricket was over at a ground that once attracted crowds of up to 14,000. 'There used to be queues all the way down the road for the trolley buses and the pavements were so packed that people would spill out on to the road,' recalls David Lockwood, cricket correspondent of the splendidly named *Huddersfield Examiner*. 'Temporary seating was installed around most of the perimeter,' he adds, pointing to the track that accommodated cyclists as well as runners from the athletic club. 'The crowd was very much on top of the action.'

Even club matches used to draw between four and six thousand, particularly for knockout cup competitions. Being Yorkshire cricket watchers, they were never shy about voicing their opinions. 'I remember a Holmfirth all-rounder called Mike Bocarrow, normally a big hitter, getting bogged down towards the end of a match against Elland,' David smiles. 'Somebody shouted, "Hit the bloody ball, Bocarrow," at which point he flung his bat all the way to the running track at the rugby end and bawled back: "You foocking try it." It was a hell of a throw and the crowd roared with laughter.'

But his abiding memory is of Geoff Boycott hitting a six out of the ground. Not an everyday occurrence, it must be said. 'He was quite circumspect getting to his century,'

David confirms. 'But then he'd crack on.' In this case, he cracked the ball all the way over the Spaines Road end and into the street beyond. It came to rest against a church door. The Sunday League opponents on that occasion, in June 1974, were Northamptonshire, and Boycott's unfamiliar burst of flamboyance presumably hap-

pened before the unexpected loss of his contact lens in the outfield. Hundreds of spectators joined in the search, to no avail.

'He promptly bought some spares the following day,' says Tony Hutton, the inveterate cricket blogger who has been hooked on the game ever since he saw another great Yorkshire and England opener, his name-sake Len, accumulating a century at Fartown in 1948. Again the opponents were Northants, who were all out for 180 on the final Friday morning, the left-arm spin-ner Johnny Wardle having taken 6 for 67. Yorkshire required 167 to win. 'They didn't race to victory; they strolled to victory,' Tony recalls. 'It took the openers seventy overs and five balls to reach their target.' Hutton was exactly 100 not out. His namesake had just taken his eleven-plus and noted with schoolboy amuse-ment some of the names on a scorecard that's still in his possession. The Northants team included Garlick and Nutter, with one Ken Fiddling behind the stumps.

'At least no Yorkshire batsman fell to what seemed to me the hilarious combina-tion of caught Fiddling bowled Nutter,' says Tony, now seventy-three and happy to turn the clock back.

▼ The overgrown terrace in front of the former pavilion is today a melancholy contrast to the packed crowd of earlier days (inset).

Yorkshire against Worcester at Fartown on 20 May 1953. Opening batsmen Len Hutton and Harry Halliday walk out to the crease.

33: IMPERIAL TOBACCO

Back in 1988, one of the greatest bowlers of all time travelled right across the globe to play for a season at the Imperial (Tobacco) Athletic Club's ground in Bristol. Admittedly, nobody had heard of Shane Warne in those days. He was eighteen and it wasn't immediately apparent that, five years hence, he would be able to turn a cricket ball twice the width of Mike Gatting. We'll let another Mike, better known to his mates as Micky Hall, take up the story. He was Imperial's coach at the time, having played for the first XI with distinction since 1960. Over to you, Micky:

'Well, I picked him up from the station and he had tea with us at our house. Nice kid he was. Bit of a Jack-the-lad but friendly enough. He stayed in the former groundsman's flat above the old pavilion. When the wind blew, it creaked a bit and he swore there was a ghost in there. My wife let him have some blankets. She asked me what kind of cricketer he was after he'd been here a day or two and I'd had chance to have a look at him in the nets. "I'll tell you what," I told her. "He'll make a better batsman than bowler."'

Micky tells the story against himself with good grace. Former team-mates and colleagues gathered round a table in the clubhouse of what is now the South Bristol Sports Centre have heard it before, but it never fails to raise a smile. Like Bristol itself, the company is fairly evenly divided between supporters of Gloucestershire and those of Somerset. Although Gloucester's County Ground is under five miles away, we're currently south of the Avon down Somerset way. The county played first-class fixtures here from 1957 to 1966 and John Player League matches from 1971 until 1979.

'I remember coming to see Viv Richards bat,' says Roger Neck, vice-chairman of the Bristol and District Cricket League. 'It was one of the biggest disappointments of my life.

◀◀ The Imperial Athletic Ground's magnificent 1908 pavilion ablaze on the night of 17 March 1999.

▲ The blackened skeleton after the disastrous fire.

He came in at the non-striker's end and was backing up when a freak shot hit the bowler's hand and was diverted on to the stumps, running him out. I remember Viv walking off with his bat over his shoulder, laughing his head off.'

Peter Lewis wasn't laughing when he came in to bat against Richards' bowling. 'Viv was playing for Lansdown [Bath] while going through his qualification period for Somerset, and he was on a hat-trick. Sent down the quickest off-break I've ever seen, but I managed to block it.' And how many did you go on to get? 'Can't remember.' He can't remember bowling his own off-breaks to Richards either. Or perhaps he's blotted out the memory, like a lot of bowlers had to after watching their finest deliveries disappearing over long on or mid wicket. Bowling to the great man on a plum batting wicket such as Imperial's must have been a trying experience.

 The campaign to save the Imperial Athletic Ground from redevelopment was unsuccessful: today the site of the pavilion is housing.

▼ Somerset playing Northants at Imperial Tobacco's Bristol ground in July 1963.

'Best wicket in the West Country George Emmett called it,' says Micky. Wasn't he a Gloucestershire player? 'He was. But he came here as manager when he retired from first-class cricket. He had a grace-and-favour house at the far end of the ground.'

That far end is just about visible, separated from the clubhouse as it is by a substantial acreage of flattish fields. Between here and there are football pitches, tennis courts, hockey pitches, bowling greens – just about every sporting surface you can think of apart from a cricket pitch. Yet there were no fewer than six squares here at one time and six groundsmen to go with them. (Warne worked on the ground staff when he wasn't rewriting the Western League record books for the most wickets in a season.)

'You'd sometimes have five games going on any Saturday afternoon,' says former second team wicketkeeper, club secretary and treasurer Peter Tucker, 'although more often it was four.'

'And sometimes a ladies' team as well,' someone reminds him. As long ago as 1905, an edict was issued to employees of what was then W.D. and H.O. Wills that one of the new pitches being laid out on 23.7 acres of pasture land would be 'reserved for women and girls, if a sufficient number wish to play'. For much of the twentieth century, the company would continue to uphold what Bob Harragan in his book *Cricket Grounds of Somerset* called 'the ethos of keeping a big workforce healthy in mind and

◀ A young Shane Warne once shivered in the first-floor flat at the top of the pavilion.

body'. As a cigarette company – the manufacturers of Woodbines, among others – they were hardly improving the health of the nation as a whole. But then few practitioners of medical science would have been aware of that until the second half of the century.

Behind us on the clubhouse wall is a picture of the magnificent pavilion that opened in time for the 1908 season. It was here, in the spacious top-floor flat, that young Warne spent his first sleepless night in Bristol eighty years on. The building was 88ft long and 50ft deep with a veranda running the length of the first storey. Belgian refugees were housed there during the First World War and a squadron of Royal Gloucestershire Hussars for the early part of the Second. By the time my current companions were in their cricketing prime, the 1960s and '70s, the pavilion's interior could have done with a little updating. 'The building was priceless to look at but useless to be inside,' Peter Tucker recalls, before deciding: 'Perhaps that's a little strong. Let's just say it had become rather Spartan with concrete floors, wooden benches and big, old-fashioned showers.'

We troop outside to take a look at where it once stood, right at the far end of the fields from the site of George Emmett's house. And we gaze out towards cover point and deep extra cover where a row of town houses now stands, inevitably christened The Pavilions by Hanson Properties. Lord Hanson had bought the ground from Imperial in the early 1990s. No paternalist he, support for sport in general and the time-consuming business of cricket in particular, seeped away. Imperial CC left the ground at the end of 1996, played for one season at the home of Fry's Chocolate and folded the following year.

And that magnificent pavilion? Well, Bristol City Council was apparently working towards having the building listed when it burnt down in a fire on the night of 17 March 1999. The elm trees that once fringed the ground had been chopped down some years previously.

Imperial's is hardly the only cricket ground in the immediate area to disappear over the past quarter of a century or so. There were three within not much more than a huge Viv Richards six from here. Robertson's Jam was one; George's, later Courage Brewery, another.

We're standing with our backs to what was, in pre-Beeching days, a railway line linking Bristol to the coal fields of north Somerset. It was inevitably known as the railway end and, if the 4.15 passed behind the sight screen at a critical moment, the umpire would signal whoever was bowling to pause in his run-up. Another case of train stopped play, perhaps. But what really stopped play here and at grounds elsewhere in Bristol, and indeed in cities all over the land, was the death of paternalism and that quaint idea that even cigarette companies had an obligation to keep their workforce 'healthy in mind and body'.

IMPERIAL
TOBACCO

167

The Imperial ground in happier days.

34: KIRKCALDY

Outside Scotland, Kirkcaldy is known as the home of Raith Rovers and Gordon Brown, but not necessarily in that order. As a lad, young Gordon apparently sold programmes outside the evocatively named Stark's Park in return for free entry to watch his beloved Rovers. He also played rugby. Indeed it was an end-of-term match for Kirkcaldy High School that resulted in the injury that would eventually lead him to lose the sight of one eye. That fateful game was played at Beveridge Park, a recreation ground that was also the home of Kirkcaldy Cricket Club from 1856 for just over a century.

If Brown was interested in cricket, he kept it well hidden. He would have been seven when Kirkcaldy CC moved to what would become their home turf for the next thirty-four years. There were no sightings of our future Prime Minister reading Locke's *Treatise on Civil Government* between overs at Bennochy, as the new ground was known. It was officially opened, on 7 June 1958, by Mrs R. Wemyss Honeyman, who – sporting a spotted two-piece and a formidable hat – cut a tape in front of the pavilion. The following year, Kirkcaldy unearthed a formidable talent in the shape of seventeen-year-old Alan Ormrod, who would go on to forge a long and successful career with Worcestershire.

Certainly he matured better than the pavilion. According to club historian David Potter, 'it was OK but aged rather quickly.' At least the bar functioned efficiently enough on match days, when carousing went on long into the night. 'There were some houses around the ground, but they weren't close enough for anyone to complain about the noise,' he continues.

David himself played for the second team in the 1970s – 'briefly and badly', as he puts it on the back of his book *A Long Innings: The Story of Kirkcaldy Cricket Club*. He then became an umpire and well remembers 'absolutely bitter days' at the beginning of each season when sea breezes blew with the strength of a gale and bowlers would hand him two sweaters before coming in to bowl from the town end or the Bennochy Road end. Two sleeveless sweaters stayed put.

'The ground was on a plateau and quite high up,' he points out. A good place, it seems, for a succession of West Indian professionals to acclimatise themselves to British conditions. If they could play here in May, a chilly day at Derby or Weston-super-Mare would seem almost balmy by comparison. Among the pros that Kirkcaldy attracted were Gus Logie of Trinidad and Tobago and the West Indies, and Ray Joseph of Guyana, who would eventually turn out for Scotland.

As summers in Kirkcaldy wore on, the sweaters were peeled off. David remembers the sun glinting on the sea, clearly visible from one boundary, and the chimes of ice cream vans trying to tempt the sparsely spread spectators. When money went missing from the pavilion one day, it was easy to spot the 'wrong 'uns'. Or so it seemed when demon left-arm fast bowler Brian Diach, a PE teacher built like the proverbial village blacksmith, had two youths pinned to a tree. They were duly frisked, but no money was found in their pockets. 'That's because they'd hidden it behind the cistern in the gents,' David recalls. 'They were caught sneaking back in later on.'

His old friend David Leitch, Cricket Scotland historian and scorer for the Royal High Club in Edinburgh, remembers a match in the early 1980s when he and some intrepid supporters travelled to Kirkcaldy by public transport so that they could enjoy to the full the post-match hospitality. 'It took us over two hours by a circuitous route involving bus, ferry over the Firth of Forth, train and taxi – only to discover that all bar three of our players had been stuck in traffic congestion on the Forth Road Bridge. Our captain, Rolly Crawford, was one of the three who made it on time and he had no option but to bat. He and his fellow opener proceeded to block with great aplomb for thirty minutes until reinforcements arrived.'

That was no mean achievement against a side like Kirkcaldy. In 1984, they won the East of Scotland League for the first time – and the only time, as it happens, although the club continued to prosper during the '80s. Which makes their decline and fall during the '90s all the more difficult and painful for David to analyse. 'For one reason or another, player after player left the club and enthusiasm dropped,' he writes. Even the bar ('the mainstay of most Scottish clubs', as he puts it) began to run at a loss with fewer people around. But the main reason was that a developer made the owner of the Bennochy ground an offer he was keen to accept. Houses and a doctor's surgery now stand on the site. 'I was diagnosed with arthritis and the need for a hip replacement near the spot where I used to sit happily on the boundary, keeping the score,' David goes on.

The club moved back to Beveridge Park, where it limped on for a few more years. Kirkcaldy's final withdrawal from the league came just before the 1997 season, a little over two weeks before the town's best-known son strode into Number 11 Downing Street.

▲ Clearing rain water from the Bennochy pitch in 1985.

35: CASTLETON

We are in Sparth Bottoms, Rochdale, and it's raining. Not an unusual state of affairs, I'm told. Rain stopped play for good during Castleton Cricket Club's last home fixture here. The date was 14 August 1965, and Whalley Range from nearby Manchester had scored 49 for 2, chasing 149 for victory. John Raby knows the statistics only too well, as he recently discovered the score book at the bottom of a drawer at home. 'I find that I made 69 not out,' he says, rolling back the years to a time when he was twenty-eight and in his prime. His wan smile is like a little ray of sunshine in the prevailing gloom.

Sparth Bottoms, as the name suggests, is at the bottom end of town. Behind us is a car breaker's yard and the red-brick chimney of a derelict mill. Ahead is the industrial estate built over what was once the poshest cricket club in Rochdale. 'We were known as Castleton Gentlemen,' John recalls. 'Apart from me and my father [both clerks], the team was largely made up of professional types – solicitors, doctors, dentists and the like.' The Chief Constable, one Major Joe Harvey, opened the batting and once gave young John a lift to the ground in his Jaguar while sporting his full dress uniform.

The gentlemanly traditions went all the way back to the previous century and almost certainly accounted for Lancashire's decision in 1876 to bestow on Castleton only the second first-class match outside Old Trafford since the formation of the county club twelve years previously. Three 'gents', Messrs E.L. Chadwick, J. Leach and J. Schofield, not only put up the financial guarantee to the Lancashire committee; they also played in a Lancashire side that included seven amateurs.

The crowd on that occasion was rather more proletarian than the players, with the workforces of local mills and tanneries well represented. Kent were shot out for 56 in their first innings and only Lord Harris, with 82, offered much resistance in the second. They may, however, have been put off their stroke by the strident tones of the Healey Hall Prize Band, which played incessantly behind the scoring tent. The music could well have hindered the scorer as well, as the umpires apparently shouted rather than signalled their decisions. Anyway, Lancashire won by ten wickets and the game was all over by 4.30 on the second day. 'The guarantors were forced to stand the loss,' write Malcolm Lorimer and Don Ambrose in their book *Cricket Grounds of Lancashire*, 'and the club and Rochdale were never again to be graced by a first-class fixture.'

The Castleton wicket was considered too soft. 'Teams from Manchester, used to firmer tracks, were still complaining about that in my day,' John confirms. 'As if there wasn't enough rain already, there was a groundsman who got up early to "roll the dew" into the wicket.' So did it turn a bit when the sun came out? 'It did, but very slowly.'

The Rabys, senior and junior, seemed to prosper on it, however. 'Dad and me once put on 50 for the last wicket against Bolton,' John confides. 'But he got out for 23 and we lost. I never let him forget that. I was 28 not out at the end. It was my GCE biology exam the next day, but I'd had two pints after the match. That was more than enough for a sixteen-year-old and I reckon that's why I failed.'

The bar was in a corner of a pavilion with a certain faded grandeur. It was single-storey, with glass doors that could be slid back on those rare occasions when the sun made an appearance. 'The showers were a bit primitive and you'd sometimes find the occasional empty beer barrel in there,' John remembers. But it's evident that he loved the ground, whether he was batting or running in with his fast-medium deliveries from either the Sparth Bottoms end or the Manchester Road end.

As the 1950s gave way to the 1960s, however, not enough youngsters like John were coming through the ranks and Castleton was struggling to put out one team, let alone two. Closure was inevitable. Rochdale FC used the site as its training ground for a while before the land was sold off for industrial development. For John Raby, still young and keen, it was time to step up a league. After a short spell with Cheetham Hill in Manchester, he moved just down the road to play for Rochdale CC in the very competitive Central Lancashire League. 'It was like moving from rugby union in the amateur days to rugby league,' he says.

Anything but gentlemanly.

◀ The Castleton team of circa 1958 in front of the pavilion.

36: ROCHDALE

A sudden chill descends as we approach what used to be the square at Rochdale Cricket Club's former ground. But then we are walking between the freezers in Asda on the way to the cooked meats counter. There's something ironically appropriate about that. After all, the pitch had been laid out on Butcher Meadow when it opened for business in 1878 with a game between 'Twenty of Rochdale' and the United South of England XI. Yes, the Grace brothers were there and W.G. took part in the opening ceremony. But, as the years went on, the ground began to look less and less meadow-like and became known as plain Dane Street.

'This is about where the main wicket was,' says Rochdale secretary Alistair Bolingbroke, taking imaginary guard within a few feet of some glistening coils of Lancashire black pudding. 'Oops, sorry, love,' he mutters a few seconds later as he's forced to step aside for a well-laden trolley being pushed purposefully by a young woman in a hurry. Undeterred, Alistair continues to explain that the wicket ran not quite east to west. 'The sun went down over mid off.'

John Raby nods agreement and reminds his old team-mate that there was 'a dark, satanic mill' at one end. 'We used to have to pay some young lad to climb over the wall and get the ball back. But by that time the building was used by a company that laid electricity cables, so it was known as the electricity end.' (There's a gas holder in another corner of what was once Rochdale's ground, but it's not quite on the scale of those at The Oval.)

John, seventy-three, came here in the late 1960s, soon after the closure of the nearby Castleton Club. Alistair is twelve years his junior and the two have been joshing each other all morning about the respective merits of their batting. Yet both would have required technique and grit to cope with the sort of bowling that they had to face. The Central Lancashire League has had more than its fair share of professionals, young and old, capable of putting the ball in the right place and making it do something.

◄◄ Frank Bolingbroke, groundsman at Dane Street, with what was regarded as the 'light' roller.

Colin Croft gave Alistair a particularly hard time on one occasion, but he still managed to come away with a fifty. As for John, he once took 21 off an over from Joel Garner. 'He was a young lad on the way up at the time,' he shrugs. 'I wouldn't have wanted to face him once he'd got that run-up sorted out.' On another occasion, he hit Roy Gilchrist for six fours in an eight-ball over. 'But he was on the way down.' Then there was Sonny Ramadhin. 'I played with him and against him,' says John. 'He didn't get me out, but he did tie me down. And he was getting on a bit by that time. Lovely man. Our captain, Ken Grieves, brought him in to play for Rochdale on one occasion. We lost, but he still managed to get four wickets.'

Pros at Rochdale in the distant past included Sydney Barnes and Sir Learie Constantine. The 1950s brought Charlie Barnett, once of Gloucestershire and England, and Dattu Phadkur, once of Bombay and India. But the biggest draw of all was Sir Garfield Sobers, who played here as pro for visiting Littleborough. 'There was a large crowd, as you might expect,' Alistair recalls, 'and the club cashed in with a raffle. The bloke who organised it wanted Sobers to draw the winning number and sent someone to find him. He couldn't have known much about cricket because he barged into the visitors' dressing room and called out: "Which one of you lot is Sobers?"'

The great man's response is not recorded.

Dane Street played host to some big crowds, particularly in the 1920s, as the accompanying picture confirms. 'I think that was taken on a Whit Monday,' Alistair suggests. 'But they were still packing them in here on occasions in the '50s. When I was a kid, there was a uniformed commissionaire with medals stopping anybody but members getting into the pavilion enclosure.'

The pavilion stood on a site now partially occupied by one of the trolley bays in Asda's car park. What was the building like?

'Much the same as the one down the road at Castleton,' says Alistair. 'They were both fine when they were built, but gradually disintegrated with minimal improvement.' By 1994 the heady days of big crowds paying hard-earned 'brass' to watch club cricket had long gone and, as Rochdale's financial plight grew, a special offer from Asda to buy the site was viewed as impossible to turn down. 'There was a covenant on Dane Street that cricket should be played there in perpetuity,' Alistair admits. 'But if we hadn't accepted the offer, there wouldn't be a Rochdale Cricket Club now.'

The new ground is 'a three-iron shot away' from what was once Butcher Meadow on the site of a former school. Yes, the school had playing fields, but no, it didn't have a cricket pitch. 'As supermarkets take over cricket grounds,' John observes dryly, 'so clubs take over school grounds.' Such is the dearth of cricket in state schools that if the clubs didn't take on responsibility for bringing on youngsters, the future of the game in England would be dead meat.

37: LAKENHAM

Lakenham was part of the fabric of Norwich – built with mustard money (Colman's, of course) and based on Cricket Ground Road. At one time they could have renamed it Tennis Court Way. But there was always something rather transitory about the inflated structures housing indoor tennis that mushroomed on the site where Norfolk played from 1879 until the turn of the twenty-first century. 'Two enormous balloon-like tents' that 'presumably make pots of money' was how Henry Blofeld described them with evident distaste in the *Independent* of 11 August 2000.

Blowers had been back to report on the last rites at his beloved county ground the day before. Norfolk had lost to Cheshire, the home side's cause not helped by the loss of their fastest bowler and number three batsman Steve Goldsmith through an unfortunate accident. He had, apparently, hurt his back before breakfast while pulling on his socks. 'The cricket gods pay no heed to sentiment,' *Test Match Special*'s bus-spotting pigeon fancier reflected, before evoking some of the ghosts who graced this ground in happier times.

Grace himself turned up here, needless to say, albeit not until 1902 when his London Counties side came to town. Then there was the father-figure of Norfolk cricket, Mike Falcon, who played for the county from before the First World War until after the Second. He scored 12,000 Minor Counties runs, including twenty-two centuries, and took 739 wickets. On fifty-six occasions he took more than five in an innings. What's more, he could step up a league when required. In 1921, he took eight Australian wickets for Archie MacLaren's XI at Eastbourne. They were the only side to beat the tourists that year.

179

◀◀ The scoreboard registering the current state of a once-vibrant Lakenham cricket ground.

▼ Michael Falcon leads out the Norfolk team in 1925. On the right is G.R.R. Colman, one of the mustard-making family that bankrolled the Lakenham ground.

▶ The Norfolk team that played Hertfordshire in 1908.

'I well remember going out with Falcon to the middle at Lakenham as a boy during one lunch interval,' Blowers writes. 'The great man used his shooting stick to show me where none other than S.F. Barnes would pitch the ball when bowling for Staffordshire. He was so accurate that at the end of an innings, when he had bowled 20 or 30 overs, there would be a small, round, bare patch exactly on a good length.'

In the post-war years, the road from Lakenham to Lord's would be well trodden. Peter Parfitt and, later, Clive Radley started their careers at Norfolk before moving to Middlesex. John Edrich got as far as The Oval, where he turned out for Surrey, while his cousin Bill played for Norfolk either side of his distinguished Middlesex career. He came back from Lord's to Lakenham as captain in 1959, and went on until well into his fifties.

Blofeld remembers him catching most things at first slip as well as being a 'considerable conversationalist'. And he should know. Young Henry was behind the stumps when old Bill came back to Norfolk. 'Blofeld was sixteen when he first played wicketkeeper for us,' says his old friend David Armstrong. 'I also remember him getting a couple of fifties as an opening bat.'

There's not much that David doesn't remember about cricket at Lakenham. Now in his mid-seventies, he was in a Moses basket when he was first taken to the ground by his father, a clergyman who had married late in life. 'Dad was old enough to recall going to his first game there in 1893. He loved the place and so did I. It was my idea of heaven. Apart from National Service, I didn't miss a home game from 1949 until it closed.' What about work? 'I was a school teacher, so I was off for most of the summer.'

▼ A match at Lakenham on a drizzly day in 1912.

He always sat in the same place – next to the sight screen at what was known as the nets end, opposite the bowling green end. 'I remember somebody parking his car behind that screen on the assumption that it would be quite safe there. Unfortunately for him, Bill Edrich cleared the screen with a six that landed straight on the roof with a resounding clatter.' Not surprisingly, perhaps, Edriches feature prominently in the Armstrong memory bank. 'Bill's brother Eric was on 98 against Kent seconds in 1949

▼ A match in 1950, as seen from the pavilion at Lakenham.

when a cow escaped from the livestock market and held up play for fifteen minutes. At one point it became wedged in the gents and was pretty frisky when it managed to get out again. Spectators fled in all directions. As I recall, the *Eastern Daily Press* described the steps of the scoreboard as more crowded than a bus on a Bank Holiday Monday. Pursued by drovers on bikes, the cow leapt over a fence and was finally brought to ground on some nearby allotments. Colin Cowdrey played in that match and he had a good laugh about it when I met up with him years later.'

Heavenly days indeed. David briefly became club scorer for two matches before going on to become club secretary and then president for four years. These days he lives on the Norfolk coast with his wife, Gail, who went with him to many a match at Lakenham. Despite their deep affection for the place, they can understand why it had to close and why Norfolk had to move on to their present ground at Horsford on the other side of the city. 'Conditions had deteriorated,' he says, 'to the point where it had become embarrassing to entertain visiting teams.'

Never more so than early in the 1996 and '97 seasons when Norfolk hosted two Benson and Hedges Cup games. 'Warwickshire came first, then Lancashire,' recalls current club secretary Stephen Skinner. 'Brian Lara was captain of one and Mike Atherton the other, and the toilets in the pavilion were regurgitating everything that went down them. Nothing had been done to the place since the end of the previous season. Colman's subsidised Lakenham heavily. But that stopped when Reckitt and Colman plc sold out to a scrap dealer who wasn't interested in cricket.'

Tennis, yes. Those balloon-like, tented tennis courts appear to have all but drifted away. The pavilion, its handsome thatched roof belying a less than idyllic interior, was still standing last time anybody cared to look and the gates were locked and barred. Plans are afoot for housing and a sports centre on the site. Hopefully, future residents will become aware just why they live off Cricket Ground Road.

LAKENHAM

183

◀ The ice cream seller does good business with the visiting Sri Lanka touring side on a hot day in 1998 during their visit to Lakenham to play an ECB XI.

The England & Australian captains (W.G. Grace & W.L. Murdoch) at Sheffield Park in 1890, on the steps of Lord Sheffield's pavilion.

38: SHEFFIELD PARK

There is still hope of resurrection. Very occasionally a cricket ground is brought back from the dead. It may be a temporary phenomenon, as looks to be the case with the former Mitchells and Butlers ground in Birmingham. Or the field could be back in play for the foreseeable future – the happy fate that has recently befallen one of the great historic country house grounds, Sheffield Park in East Sussex.

A relic of the Golden Age, its most gleaming year was 1896 when Lord Sheffield's XI, including W.G. Grace and C.B. Fry, F.S. Jackson and Arthur Shrewsbury, played the touring Australians in front of a crowd estimated at 25,000. They were the fifth Aussie side since 1884 to visit what Christopher Martin-Jenkins has described as 'the Arundel of Victorian cricket'. Bountiful hospitality and a setting of 'exceptional scenic grandeur' drew them to the home of Henry North Holroyd, the third Earl of Sheffield and the man who bequeathed Australia the Sheffield Shield. He once turned out for the Gentlemen of Sussex but, unlike that other great cricketing patron of a later age, Sir Julien Cahn, his lordship knew his limits and declined to join in when the big boys came to play.

The ground went into a slow decline after Holroyd's death in 1909. Disappearing under wheat during the First World War, it was resurrected for the first time to stage village and school matches until the early years of the next war when the Canadian Army arrived. This time it vanished under Nissen huts.

John Bradford must have been one of the last people to play on the old pitch, taking part in a match in 1940 when he was eleven years old. He is eighty-two now and not in the best of health. 'He used to cycle

▼ The original scorecard sold on the ground for the match.

over from Fletching [two miles away] to deliver the newspapers to the big house,' says his daughter-in-law Debbie. 'And he once played for the local primary school against a team from Lewes. That's all he can remember.'

Debbie works at Sheffield Park for the National Trust, which has owned house and grounds since 1954. So does her husband Alan, a gardener here since leaving school at fifteen over forty years ago. 'He's more into football than cricket,' she confides. Fletching, however, remains a cricketing hotbed. You only have to look at the photographs around the walls of the Griffin Inn to realise that. The village club's several XIs long ago acquired their own ground near the church. So who were the prime movers in restoring the pitch and outfield at Sheffield Park?

Step forward the Armadillos, a hitherto itinerant team with a fair number of lawyers among them, including a sprinkling of high court judges. 'They like playing at country house grounds,' says Peter Wigan, who turned out for them a few times in his youth. He's sixty-seven now, a committee member and the key figure behind the resurrection. 'I'd heard that they'd fallen out with their most recent landlord and it struck me that it would be fun to offer them a permanent home by recreating Sheffield Park.'

Negotiations with the National Trust began in 2004. Five years later an Old England XI, managed by Jim Parks, captained by John Lever and including John Snow, took on an Australian equivalent with the likes of Dean Jones and Rodney Hogg in its ranks. It was exactly a century on from Lord Sheffield's death and, despite charges of £20 a ticket, there was a crowd of over 2,500. That was, lest we forget, a tenth of the number who turned up on the first day of that final visit by the Australians in 1896.

As Peter gets out of his car to open the gate to the ground, I try to imagine the scene as spectators flooded over the fields from the nearby station to stand five or six deep around the boundary. Lord Sheffield's guests, meanwhile, were happily ensconced in his private pavilion, a fabulously ornate affair with many echoes of the Raj about it. More West Bengal than East Sussex, you might say. As we set off up the drive, we pass the foundations of the octagonal ladies' pavilion, another monument in its day to the flamboyant extravagance of late-Victorian architecture.

Was it strictly ladies only in there? Well, not entirely. Roger Packham's book *Cricket in the Park* carries a photograph of the Prince of Wales emerging on to the

▼ Lord Sheffield's X1 v. the Australians at Sheffield Park.

veranda and seemingly about to pull on his gloves. The old rooster had been sizing up the hen house. Or so we assume. All we know for sure is that the presence of the future Edward VII was another big draw that first day, 11 May 1896.

We get out of the car and stroll across the outfield, on a grey November day 114 years on. Peter pauses to point out the holes and humps caused by the resident wildlife. 'That's a badger's,' he says, gesturing with evident distaste at a particularly deep hole. 'They mark out their territory, then poo in it. We have to spend about an hour and a half filling in before every game. Even then the ball can sometimes shoot up and hit a fielder under the chin.'

The pitch has been turned from east–west to southeast–northwest to avoid having to bat in the full glare of a setting sun. And is the pitch still as 'fiery' as it could be on

▲ W.G. Grace during his opening stand of 101 with Arthur Shrewsbury in 1893. Australian captain Jack Blackham is keeping wicket, Lord Sheffield's pavilion is in the centre.

▼ Symbol of resurrection: the Sheffield Park pavilion today.

▲ Luncheon menu for the match between an Australian X1 and the Earl of Sheffield's X1 in May, 1893.

▼ The invitation card sent by Lord Sheffield to friends for the 1893 match.

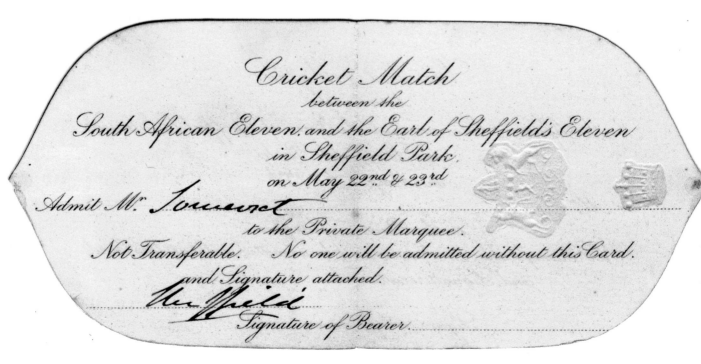

Cricket Match
between the
South African Eleven, and the Earl of Sheffield's Eleven
in Sheffield Park,
on May 22nd & 23rd

Admit Mr *Somerset*
to the Private Marquee.
Not Transferable.   No one will be admitted without this Card.
and Signature attached.

Signature of Bearer

dry days in Lord Sheffield's time? It can be, Peter assures me. 'Heaven knows what it was like to face [Fred] Spofforth when he was charging in on it.' Or, indeed, the equally fearsome Ernie (Jonah) Jones. He reputedly parted Grace's beard with his third bouncer of an over. When the great man strode down the wicket to complain, the Australian former miner grunted back: 'Sorry, Doctor, she slipped.'

As we walk back towards the car, a chilly drizzle starts to fall. But it can't quite dull the spirits that the resurrection of this evocative ground has stirred. The autumnal golds have faded as winter draws on. Six months from now, though, the rhododendrons and azaleas will be in bloom as the Armadillos take the field once more. Holes will have been filled in. Humps will have been flattened. Badgers and moles will have sniffed the wind and taken cover from the crack of willow on leather – the sound of an English summer down the ages to Lord Sheffield's day and beyond.

▲ The cover of Lord Sheffield's invitation card.

ENGLAND v. AUSTRALIA,

At Lord Sheffield's Picturesque Country Seat.

His Lordship, with his usual unbounded generosity, grants Free Admission to the General Public.

MONDAY, MAY 8th, 1893.

The Opening Struggle.

MANY young friends, many elders
　　Mingle in this happy throng,
Firm admirers of our Pastime
　　Gather in their thousands strong.
Let us hope this opening struggle
　　Will so entertain and please,
That you'll live to talk it over
　　When you're seated at your ease.
Gains are intermix'd with losses,
　　But the bitter makes the sweet,
Stony roads make common carpets
　　Seem like velvet to the feet.
If the lads of merrie England
　　Fail to beat their friendly foe,
They will, like all true born Britons,
　　Yearn to have another go.
There's a mighty work before you,
　　Keen supporters urge you on,
May it grace the page of hist'ry
　　When the year has waned and gone,
Heroes of our dear old country
　　Put your shoulders to the wheel
Make one grand united effort
　　Victory will reward your zeal.
May old Father Time prove a jolly good sort,
By sparing all friends of our national sport,
May he prove a generous and kindly old man
By sparing our players as long as he can.　**A.C.**

◀ An Albert Craig poem given away to the crowds during matches at Sheffield Park.

Cricket on the frozen lake at Sheffield Park in 1891.

BIBLIOGRAPHY

Association of Cricket Statisticians, *Cricket Grounds of …* series, various dates

Brodribb, Gerald, *Cricket at Hastings: The Story of a Ground*, Spellmount, 2009

Chalke, Stephen, *Tom Cartwright: The Flame Still Burns*, Fairfield Books, 2007

Hamilton, Duncan, *Harold Larwood*, Quercus, 2009

Hamilton, Duncan (Ed.), *Sweet Summers: The Classic Cricket Writing of J.M. Kilburn*, Great Northern Books, 2007

Johnson, Martyn and Christine, *Wentworth Postcard Memories*, self-published, 2010

Moulton, Roger, *Joe Hardstaff: Supreme Stylist*, Lives in Cricket series, Association of Cricket Statisticians, 2010

Packham, Roger, *Cricket in the Park: The Life and Times of Lord Sheffield (1832–1909)*, Methuen, 2009

Potter, David, *A Long Innings: The Story of Kirkcaldy Cricket Club*, McGilvray Printers, 2010

Rae, Simon, *W.G. Grace: A Life*, Faber & Faber, 1998

Rijks, Miranda, *The Eccentric Entrepreneur: A Biography of Sir Julien Cahn*, The History Press, 2008

Ulyatt, Mike, *See You Down at the Circle*, Mike Ulyatt Enterprises, 2004

Varley, Robin A., *'All That Could Be Desired': History of Cricket in Aberystwyth 1830–1997* Cambrian Printers, 2004

INDEX

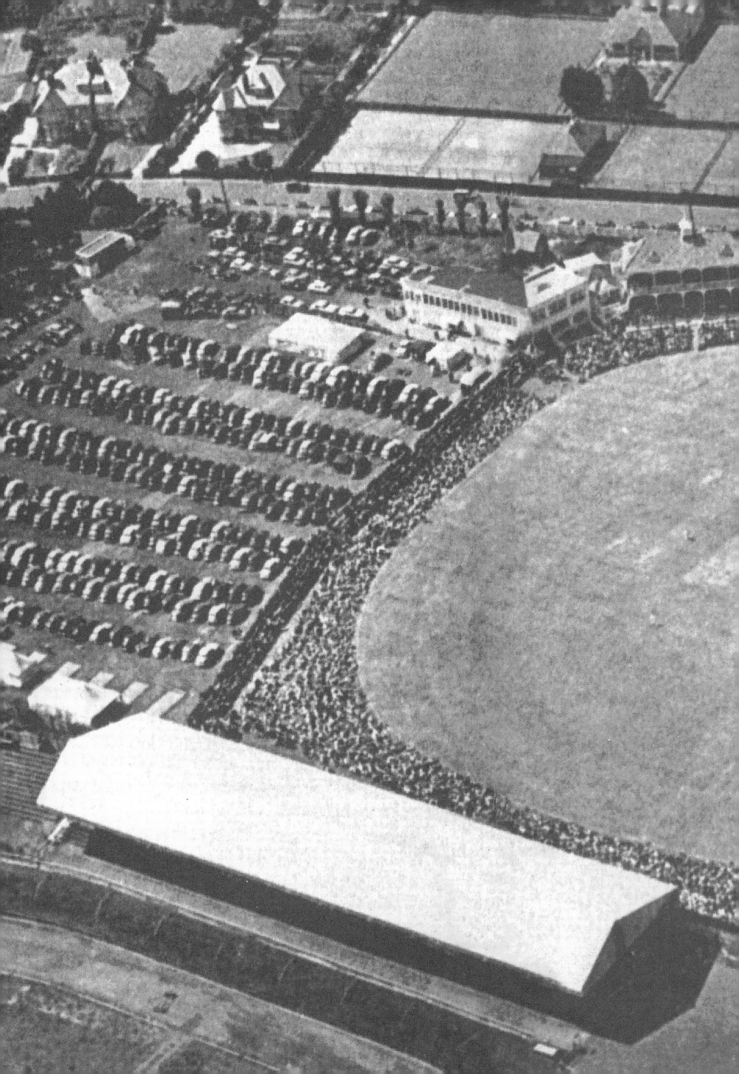